THE OFFICIAL GUIDE

Flight goggles
acquired on travels

Vandor frost
clings to coat

CHEWBACCA

THE OFFICIAL GUIDE

WRITTEN BY **PABLO HIDALGO**

CONTENTS

FOREWORD

It's 1988 and I'm nine years old. My mom and I are in San Francisco, seeing the sights. Golden Gate Bridge, Alcatraz, eating dim sum in Chinatown. And there's one other stop on our tour. A few years earlier, my dad had done some writing for this guy, George Lucas. *The Star Wars* guy. That was in the early eighties, before I was old enough to really appreciate it. But their past collaboration and friendship meant my mom and I were able to arrange a visit to the visual effects company that George had founded. The name alone quickened my nine-year-old pulse. Industrial Light & Magic. The fusion of technology and fantasy. The idea that anything could be made real on a movie screen was both exhilarating and terrifying – that primal cocktail of emotions that fuels the imagination of all children.

The entrance to ILM was concealed in a nondescript storefront with blacked-out windows, like a top-secret government lab. My mom and I got the tour, visiting each department; make-up effects, where I got to try on a mask for the highly anticipated *Ghostbusters* sequel; the camera department, where they were busy inventing new equipment; matte painting, that wondrous (and now sadly lost) art by which entire worlds were created with paint and ink to be indistinguishable from a photograph; and finally, the department I was most excited about: the model shop, where creatures, spaceships, sometimes even whole towns were built on the same scale as the action figures I played with on the floor of my bedroom. And there was no question, ILM made the best toys on earth.

We also drove over to the warehouse where models were stored after use. If things go according to plan, in a few years, when George and Mellody open the Lucas Museum of Narrative Art, you'll get the chance to see some of what I saw that day – the most wondrous toy chest on earth, filled with models of the Death Star, X-wings and Mon Calamari star cruisers, rancors and Eborsisks, even a certain Lost Ark (which, incidentally, was not in a wooden crate marked "TOP SECRET/ARMY INTEL" but just sitting there on a shelf gathering dust). What I felt that day, wandering through that dark, quiet warehouse, was pure wonder. What I understood, for the first time in my life, was this: imagination is magic and magic is real.

With the insight of author Pablo Hidalgo and the help of the Lucasfilm image archive, DK's books are a little like that ILM toy chest I visited as a child. They are grimoires of magic, an access point to another galaxy, one that's growing larger, richer, more dangerous, more beautiful and more real every day. Enjoy it, reference it, devour the details, but be warned, the study of magic is serious business. It will lead you to dark corners of distant worlds, places no one else has ever visited. And before you know it, you're a magician too.

At least, that's what happened to me.

JON KASDAN
Co-Writer on *Solo: A Star Wars Story*

INTRODUCTION

Solo: A Star Wars Story takes place during a dark time in the galaxy. The Jedi are gone and the merciless forces of the Empire maintain order. As the Empire expands into new territories, it encounters the operations of dangerous criminal syndicates. This book is your guide to Han Solo's adventures as he first enters this larger world. Discover the places, faces and things that Han encounters on that journey – from those that will take centre-stage and play pivotal roles in his life, to the strange dangers lurking deep in the shadows.

HEAD IN THE STARS
Under Imperial rule, the shipbuilding planet of Corellia has become a place of poverty and gang warfare. On these mean streets, a teenager named Han fights for survival but yearns to fly among the stars…

A TIMELINE OF TROUBLE
Han is cagey on the details of his own past, particularly his early childhood. His lifetime has coincided with a noteworthy period in galactic history. He was born towards the tail end of the Galactic Republic – a thousand-year institution that war transformed into the Galactic Empire. The Empire proceeded to crack down on the very freedoms it had promised its citizens.

A Separatist crisis escalates, threatening to split the Republic.

Estimated date of Han's birth on Corellia.

Around this time, Han joins up with the White Worms gang as a scrumrat.

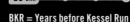

| 25 BKR | | | 20 BKR | | | | | 15 BKR |

BKR = Years before Kessel Run

The Clone Wars erupt.
The Separatist Alliance
fights for independence,
pitting its droid forces
against the Republic's
clone troopers.

The Galactic Empire sweeps into power,
riding a wave of goodwill after ending
the violence of the Clone Wars.

Former Chancellor of the Galactic
Republic, Sheev Palpatine, declares
himself Galactic Emperor.

Han is drummed out of the Navy and
sent to battlefield army duty on
Mimban, where he meets Beckett's
gang and the Wookiee Chewbacca.

Chewbacca serves in
defence of his home
planet, Kashyyyk.

The Empire begins its military
expansion, phasing out clones for
patriotic recruits and turning civilian
shipyards into military factories.

Han makes his escape
from impoverished
Corellia by joining
the Imperial Navy.

Han, Chewbacca and the crew
of the *Millennium Falcon* set
an unbelievable record for
the Kessel Run.

10 BKB

5 BKB

0 BKB

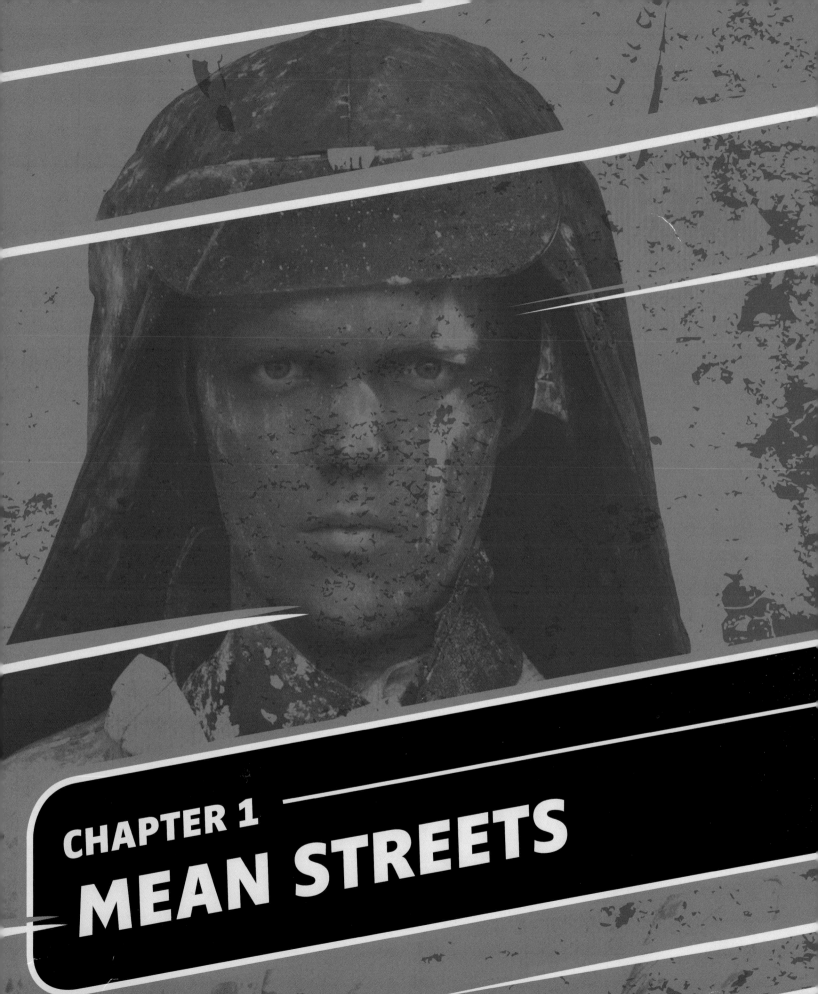

CHAPTER 1
MEAN STREETS

Santhe/Sienar Fleet Systems factory, designation Coronet-SFS-14

Desalinisation tanks extract salt from seawater for industrial use

Cooling water transfer hose

Insulated gloves with rough grip to handle slippery fish

CONTROLLED SPRAWLS

Careful land management keeps population centres from spilling out too far and turning Corellia into a city-encased planet like so many other ancient Core worlds. Coastal cities like Coronet are instead made up of island-like architectural units called pills. The oval-shaped pills are connected by waterway-spanning speeder bridges, like the Narro Sienar Boulevard.

CORELLIA

Corellia has long played a key role in the expansion of galactic civilisation. Thousands of years ago, Corellian royalty sponsored exploration and colonisation efforts that helped to spread the frontiers of the young Republic. Corellia's importance in galactic affairs has since reduced, although its historic significance remains recognised.

LIFE ON THE WATER

Long before they explored the stars, Corellians satisfied their wanderlust by voyaging across their planet's massive oceans. Sailing and fishmongering are still careers undertaken with pride, though the work is dangerous and the pay is meagre.

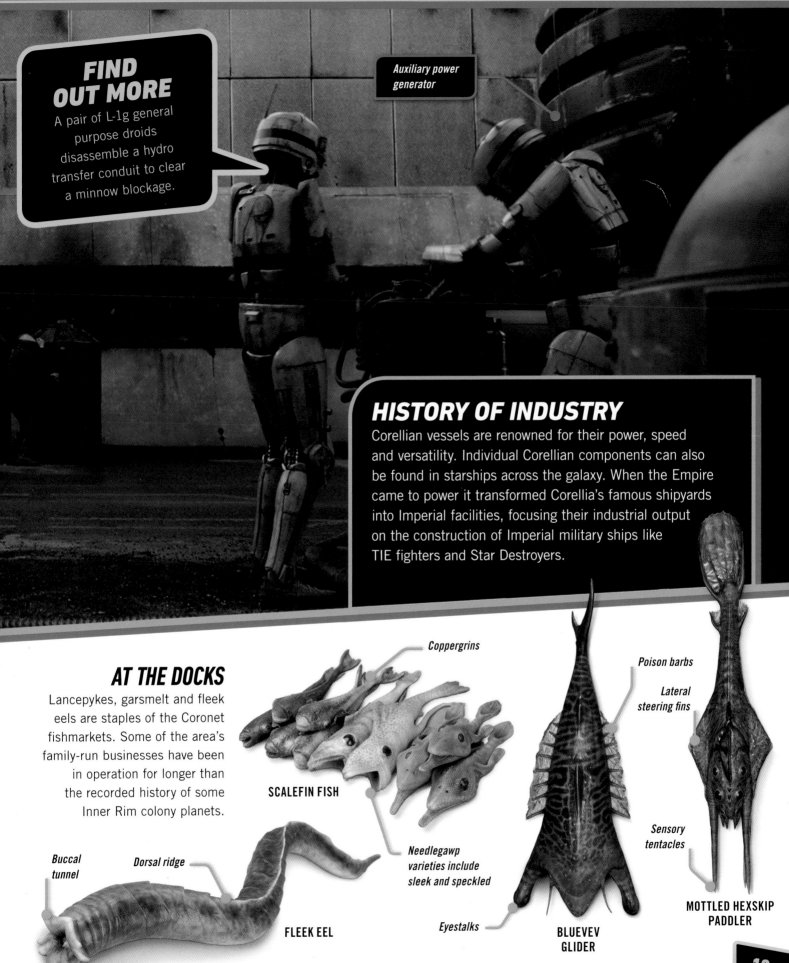

FIND OUT MORE

A pair of L-1g general purpose droids disassemble a hydro transfer conduit to clear a minnow blockage.

Auxiliary power generator

HISTORY OF INDUSTRY

Corellian vessels are renowned for their power, speed and versatility. Individual Corellian components can also be found in starships across the galaxy. When the Empire came to power it transformed Corellia's famous shipyards into Imperial facilities, focusing their industrial output on the construction of Imperial military ships like TIE fighters and Star Destroyers.

AT THE DOCKS

Lancepykes, garsmelt and fleek eels are staples of the Coronet fishmarkets. Some of the area's family-run businesses have been in operation for longer than the recorded history of some Inner Rim colony planets.

Coppergrins

Poison barbs

Lateral steering fins

SCALEFIN FISH

Sensory tentacles

Buccal tunnel

Dorsal ridge

Needlegawp varieties include sleek and speckled

Eyestalks

MOTTLED HEXSKIP PADDLER

FLEEK EEL

BLUEVEV GLIDER

IMPERIAL PATROL SPEEDER

Sprawling cities and industrial areas are common on worlds such as Corellia. In areas deemed important enough – and the valuable shipyards of Coronet certainly warrant this status – military units are increasingly taking over local law enforcement to ensure control. The Empire deploys patrol speeders piloted by specialist stormtroopers to police such environments.

Acceleration pad with positive traction field

Enhanced imaging electronics in enlarged helmet dome

Power cell access panel

Lightweight EC-17 hold-out blaster pistol

Rocker-pivoted foot pedal controls speed and altitude

BIG CITY BIKER

Patrol trooper armour allows for greater ease of movement than the full body suits worn by regular stormtroopers. This flexible uniform shares more similarities with that of scout troopers – the wilderness-based counterparts of the urban patrol troopers.

DATA FILE

MODEL Aratech C-PH patrol speeder bike

AFFILIATION Galactic Empire

HEIGHT 1.37 m (4 ft 6 in)

LENGTH 4.12 m (13 ft 6 in)

CREW 1

SPEED 400 kph (248 mph)

WEAPONS Forward fixed blaster cannon

Retractable illuminator lamp on articulated mount

STREET PILOTING

The blocky design of the Aratech C-PH is meant to convey power over agility, though the advanced repulsorlift manoeuvrability systems inside the speeder provide both. Larger than most speeders, the bike's sturdy shape makes it better able to withstand high-speed collisions with other vehicles. It also boasts sophisticated electronics to keep its rider aware of any such incoming traffic.

FIND OUT MORE

The C-PH lacks the outrigger steering vanes common on most speeder bikes. Instead, it uses a forward-facing bank of repulsorfield vector guides for manoeuvring.

BlasTech Ax-25 blaster cannon

Control handle rail slot

CORONET HIGHWAY PATROL

Patrol troopers receive almost real-time data on traffic, construction and other potential city obstacles through an in-helmet connection to their headquarters. This helps them navigate congested city environments.

Non-stop construction on Corellia is making the elite richer, but few benefits are felt by citizens like Han. Factory labourers are worked to exhaustion for little pay. Those who don't work for the Empire or mega-corporations often turn to thievery to scrape by. Abandoned industrial sites and condemned housing projects become a hotbed for criminal activity.

HAN SOLO

Times are tough under Imperial rule. Han is a street thief who works for the notorious White Worms gang, stealing goods and cutting deals on behalf of an ill-tempered crime boss. But budding pilot Han has his sights set for the stars, and soon improvises an escape from Corellia.

Naapa-tanned vest with cracking weatherproof surface

Bruising from a run-in with Kilmo, a local crook

Driving gloves improve grip when steering

Belt pouch with lockpicks

Brine-covered serge fabric trousers

Zoltwen D3x macroscope

A GOOD BLASTER
As Han Solo travels the galaxy, he relies on having a trusty blaster by his side for protection. This rugged BlasTech DL-44 is stripped of its field rifle accessories to become a hefty blaster pistol.

PRIVATE ORIGINS
Han doesn't say much about his past, suggesting that, like many of the urchins crowded in the Corellian slums, he doesn't really know it. Han's cockiness, daring and ability to take a punch have made him one of the White Worms' most capable – if unpredictable – thieves.

Scuffed engineer boots

DREAMS OF SPACE

Han's piloting skills rarely get a workout on Corellia. He leaves his homeworld for the Imperial Academy on Carida, with his desire to fly outweighing his apathy for the Empire. However, the traits that make Han an incredible pilot – including a reckless disregard for common sense in favour of trusting his instincts – work against him in the rigid structure of military life.

"NEXT TIME SOMEBODY HITS ME, I'M GONNA HIT 'EM BACK."
– HAN

DATA FILE

SUBJECT Han Solo

HOMEWORLD Corellia

SPECIES Human

AFFILIATION Formerly White Worms; Imperial Flight Academy; Imperial Army

HEIGHT 1.72 m (5 ft 8 in)

ID storage tag is kept empty

Electronically shielded pocket for unprotected data cards

FIND OUT MORE

Han grows to favour a gunslinger's belt and holster that allow for a quick draw in situations where he must make an instant life or death decision.

Nerf-leather jacket

Cautionary pulser in blaster handle buzzes when low on ammo

M-68 LANDSPEEDER

Han won't admit how he ended up piloting this overpowered M-68 landspeeder. All he'll say is that its previous owner no longer had need of it. Han has a keen eye for technology, and recognises the M-68's capabilities at a glance. A simple bit of hotwiring, and it is his to take for a spin.

HIGH-PERFORMANCE VEHICLE

The landspeeder is lifted off the ground by a repulsorfield, while propulsion thrusters push the vehicle forward. Each thruster has a variable exhaust nozzle that shapes and directs thrust and lets the pilot spin the vehicle around at fast speeds. The repulsorfield also works as a traction field for better control.

FIND OUT MORE
Air is drawn into the speeder's custom cool-burning injectrine engines through a large exposed inlet on the front grill.

Exposed cooling fan for repulsorlift generator

Repulsorfield transmitter banks

Airspeed tracker and telemetry antenna

Exhaust nozzle adjusts to change direction of force

DATA FILE

MODEL Mobquet
M-68 landspeeder

AFFILIATION Civilian craft

HEIGHT 1.29 m (4 ft 3 in)

LENGTH 3.85 m (12 ft 7 in)

CREW 1

SPEED 225 kph (140 mph)

WEAPONS None

Smooth spoiler reduces air drag

"A STREET BLASTER BOLT"

The compact M-68 is considered a classic by street racing enthusiasts. Marketed to a youth audience by Mobquet Swoops and Speeders, it is available in both hardtop and open-air models. The standard M-68 comes with a 289-hirep repulsorlift generator that can easily be modified and overcharged by thrill-seekers.

Racing-style steering wheel with cut-out handles

Side ducting, fuel lines and speed-governor mechanisms

LUCKY DICE

As a good luck charm, Han carries with him a pair of aurodium-plated chance cubes. They are used in the Corellian Spike variation of sabacc, where a roll of doubles triggers card shuffles. They soon find a home on the landspeeder's windscreen.

Face shows value of "four", one of six possible results per cube

DARK CENTRE

Stacks of outdated habitation cubes – scrap from a condemned Corellian housing project – cover the abandoned industrial site where the Worms dwell. Robust access pipes, formerly used to transform Corellian seawater into fresh water, lead from the surface into the heart of the Den. The chamber's upper windows are painted black to block sunlight reaching the light-averse Grindalids within.

FIND OUT MORE

The Den's power is drawn from an unsupervised generator bank belonging to Sienar Fleet Systems. An illegal tap was set up by scrumrats, who also maintain the supply.

Scrumrats sleep in the tunnels, close to the cistern's warmth

Crates of stolen goods are ready for sale

DEN OF THE WHITE WORMS

The White Worms form the backbone of Coronet's black market, making stolen and prohibited goods available to anyone willing to pay the steep prices set by their leader, Proxima. They work and reside in the poorest parts of the city. From the surface, their base looks like an abandoned water processing plant, with only the occasional guard hinting at what lies beneath.

Lockpick stowage

Power siphon for heating element

Bedroll

SLEEPING KIT

Steam pipes make it difficult for sensors to penetrate the Den

Tunnel floor is often damp and slippery

Watery pool is home to Proxima and her young

LADY PROXIMA

Proxima is the matriarch of the White Worms – a small number of writhing Grindalids who lord it over a pack of desperate street urchins known as scrumrats. Proxima's throne room is a briny pool in the Den's central cistern. She lurks beneath the filmy water, feeding her Grindalid hatchlings and commanding her humanoid "children".

SCRAPING BY

Whatever money the White Worms make is funnelled to Proxima. Her underlings are left to make do with scraps. Their gear is improvised, refurbished and often falling apart. Necessity has taught the scrumrats to be resourceful and given them important maintenance skills.

Fire suppression water pipe

IMPROVISED TRUNCHEON

Pump mechanism

Siphon hose

Adjustable band

FUEL LEECH PACK

HEADSET VISOR

GAME CLOTH

Despite their grim surroundings, the scrumrats are still children who enjoy games. They play with stolen cards and broken playing pieces, on a makeshift gameboard fashioned from discarded fabric.

Printing shows civic water distribution network

TRUCKSPEEDER

When gang affairs require the White Worms to travel overland, Moloch's vehicle of choice is a blocky Trast Heavy Transports A-A4B truckspeeder. The armoured transport has a noisy, powerful engine that propels it and its passengers through the streets and alleys of Coronet. A forward cage holds a pack of snarling Sibian hounds eager to hunt down Moloch's quarry.

Hound pen full of barking beasts

Driver's seat with protective roll bar

Armoured cage turns speeder into a battering ram

MOLOCH

Moloch is a Grindalid brute who answers directly to Lady Proxima – leader of the White Worms. Moloch's sense of superiority over the gang's humanoid servants is encouraged by his boss. Though he rarely speaks of it, Moloch is a spiritual being, believing in a promised afterlife of endless riches.

Squinting Grindalid eyes

Flexible, concertinaed cowl armour

Articulated faceplates

Scope with built-in luma-compensators

"SNUBBLE SPECIAL" PISTOL

Moloch favours a "snubble" – a double snub-nosed blaster pistol. It packs a powerful punch, despite having limited ammunition stores. Moloch has removed the stun setting to ensure his force is always lethal.

MOLOCH UNMASKED

The Grindalid homeworld has a dense atmosphere that filters out most light, meaning that Corellia's sunlight is dangerous to Moloch and his species. For this reason, most Grindalids tend to remain in the dark depths of the favela. Moloch is one of the few who dares venture out of the shadows, protected by customised full-seal armour.

IMPATIENT ENFORCER

Moloch thinks Proxima is too easy on Han, though he'd never say so to his dear matriarch. Moloch is sure that Han's smart mouth will inevitably get the young man killed. It seems clear to Moloch that it would be more efficient to get rid of Han sooner rather than later.

"YOU'LL NEVER KNOW HOW MUCH IT PAINS ME TO DESTROY SOMETHING AS BEAUTIFUL AS YOU."

— MOLOCH, TO QI'RA

DATA FILE

SUBJECT Moloch

HOMEWORLD Corellia

SPECIES Grindalid

AFFILIATION White Worms

HEIGHT 2 m (6 ft 7 in)

Sceptre depicting writhing scrumrats

Brine-encrusted long coat

Photosensitive skin enclosed in glove

FIND OUT MORE

From a distance, Moloch looks like a two-legged creature, but he actually has tapered tail segments. Extensive practice has enabled him to impersonate a humanoid walk.

SCRUMRATS

The scrumrats are the lowest of the underlings serving the White Worms. These orphans and urchins are plucked from the slums and given a meagre chance at survival by Proxima. For many scrumrats, progressing from lowly ratcatchers or pickpockets to trusted thugs or guards is their most realistic goal in life.

Battered pipe known as the "rat hammer"

Satchel for stolen parts

BANSEE

Bansee caught the eye of Proxima by being the best ratcatcher among the girls of her age. She is mean-spirited and a tough fighter with a scrap pipe. Clever and humourless, Bansee has the rank of Third Girl among the scrumrats, but she is eager to climb higher in the gang.

INFESTATION

The scrumrats earn their unsavoury name through the vermin-hunting duties that they all must undertake. The Den is infested with vervikks, screerats and other unwholesome critters, which the urchins hunt. Scrumrats bring the captures to Proxima's pools, where the choicest morsels are chewed up by the gang leader and fed to her baby worms.

CHATES

The son of a farmer who was tragically killed by muggers during a visit to a Coronet bank, Chates was left alone in the big city at a young age. He soon fell in with the scrumrats. Chates admires Rebolt, one of the White Worms' toughest thugs, and hopes to impress him by clobbering Han.

Portable Holonet transceiver

JAGLEO

A former dancer, Jagleo has adapted her balance and coordination into a self-invented style of martial art. The nimble thief can shimmy into tight spaces.

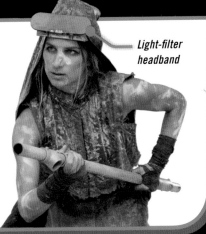

Light-filter headband

Valuable wires

TUNNEL TOLI

Little Toli earns his keep by slipping into utility wiring trunks and patching into power and data grids. This keeps the Den connected to the rest of the planet.

Work goggles with magnifying lenses

HALLON

Young Hallon can squeeze through narrow spaces to reach areas older thieves cannot. Against orders, he has been letting pests escape the Den alive.

QI'RA

Qi'ra clawed her way up from the wasteland of the Silo, using her cunning to secure a profitable deal for Lady Proxima, and earning the role of Head Girl. At age 18, Qi'ra now commands the attention and respect of Proxima, if not her full trust. Proxima admires Qi'ra's planning and strategy, but recognises a potentially threatening schemer when she sees one.

Comlink and breather mask

Twi'lek lekku

COSDRA AND LEKELF

Loyalty has afforded these older scrumrats many perks. Cosdra and LeKelf perch near the surface where they act as sentries for the Den and can enjoy slightly fresher air than that found below the surface.

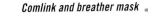

Lock-picking spikes in belt loops

Bracelet with compass

COMMANDER OF STAVES

Rebolt backs his bullying words with a bludgeoning staff he made for himself out of a snapped transmission mast with ends wrapped in leather straps. If Rebolt connects it to a power cell, the staff's conductive surfaces give it an extra jolt. He has nicknamed his club the "Commander of Staves", after the sabacc face card.

Conductive tungsten metal

Weighted end (when housing a power cell)

REBOLT'S CLUB

Insulating Rycrit leather strap, tightly wound

CORELLIAN THUGS

Moloch's favoured goons are Rebolt and Syke. The pair's competition with one another to prove who is toughest amuses the White Worm enforcer. Though Rebolt is currently the better animal handler, Syke is quickly catching up.

Protective padding

Heavy, puncture-proof hound-handling gloves

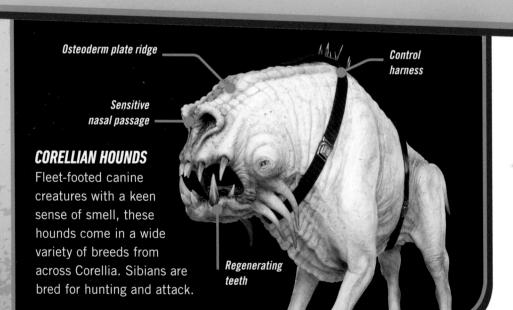

Osteoderm plate ridge

Control harness

Sensitive nasal passage

CORELLIAN HOUNDS

Fleet-footed canine creatures with a keen sense of smell, these hounds come in a wide variety of breeds from across Corellia. Sibians are bred for hunting and attack.

Regenerating teeth

Waterproof boots

SYKE

Syke shows a gentle fondness for the Sibian hounds, a trait his rival Rebolt thinks is a weakness to exploit. Someday, Syke hopes to set his favourite hound, Taomat, on Rebolt and end this petty contest.

Light-intensifying visor plate

REBOLT

An unimaginative and pitiless goon who carries out Moloch's orders unquestioningly, Rebolt is driven by ambitions that outstrip his abilities. Growing up in the Den, he aspired to one day be Proxima's Head Boy, but his attempts were repeatedly undermined by smarter scrumrats like Han and Qi'ra.

FIND OUT MORE

Thugs of a certain rank are honoured with breathing collars that fan purified air into their faces, rather than being forced to wear restrictive breathing masks.

Sealable pocket holding money, ration bar and vibro-shiv

Atmospheric treatment tubing

Brine-covered coveralls

DATA FILE

SUBJECT Rebolt

HOMEWORLD Corellia

SPECIES Human

AFFILIATION White Worms

HEIGHT 1.73 m (5 ft 8 in)

"WE'LL MAKE SURE YOU DON'T GET LOST ON YOUR WAY..."
– REBOLT TO HAN

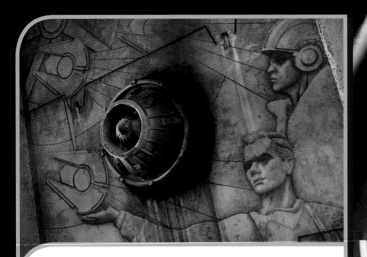

CORELLIAN VISION

The spaceport has a relief sculpture depicting the Edjian Prince, a mythical Corellian figure who braved the unknown forests of the Uhl Eharl Khoehng. Such legends predate the Old Republic and helped define the spirit of adventure and exploration that have become essential parts of Corellian heritage.

Customs booths are staffed by CorSec officers

Stormtroopers marshal crowds into long lines

Entry documentation

Exit documentation

TRAVEL DOCUMENT DATA TAGS

Tamper-proof laminate casing

Extendable antenna

CORONET SPACEPORT

An expansive facility on the city coastline, Coronet Spaceport handles the flow of civilian, military and commercial traffic in and out of Corellia. The Empire has taken over the major terminals for its needs, pushing secondary services to one of the outer pill-shaped structures that the spaceport covers.

SECURITY COMLINK

Encryption dialler

Vo-pickup microphone grill

FIND OUT MORE
Travellers wait for departing transports beyond the customs gates. An exit from Corellia is tantilisingly close for those stuck on the other side without the correct documentation.

NEW AND OLD

Imperial architecture and symbols now pervade the granite structures that have served for centuries as entry and exit points for Corellia. Banners with icons of the New Order and inspirational propaganda touting service in the Imperial Navy are impossible to avoid. For newcomers, these signs are a promise of stability and opportunity. For those leaving, it is a promise that the Empire will always be watching them.

Turnstile sensors read all ID tags within a set radius

Elevated duty station grants superior visibility

Shockproof travel case

INGRESS AND EGRESS

Security is paramount at the spaceport, since saboteurs could wreak great economic damage by targeting the vital transportation hub. Security in the spaceport used to be the sole responsibility of Corellian Security Forces (CorSec), but in recent years the Imperial military has stepped in to offer additional expertise, personnel and equipment.

TRANSIT DATA READER

Security-focused "hard" keys

Biometric scanning surface

User-defined touch-sensitive "soft" keys

Calibration nodes

Sensor conduits

BODY SCANNING WAND

A NEW START

Ballia Noaddo is one of many unhappy citizens trying to leave Corellia. She has resigned from her executive position at the Corellian Engineering Corporation, unhappy about growing Imperial influence at the company.

GALAXY TRAVELLERS

Long queues snake through the terminals of Coronet Spaceport, full of desperate travellers. Many are eager to leave the worsening conditions on Corellia, wary of the scrutiny of Imperial security and hopeful at what lies ahead. But first, they must run a gauntlet of officials who question their loyalties and motives.

Temperature-sensitive Barbadelan tendrils

Cowl trails down to attached satchels

DOBARN TREN

A priest of the Sacred Way, Dobarn Tren came to Coronet hoping to alleviate the suffering of the city's poorest residents. This drew unwanted attention from law enforcement officials, who incorrectly suspected him of buying and selling illegal wares on the black market. Rather than face deportation, Tren is regretfully volunteering to leave.

THE XOCZUKO FAMILY

Jannitha Xoczuko, a droid programmer, has been studying manufacturing processes and offering her efficiency expertise at the Corellian Engineering Corporation for the past six years. Disheartened at the gruelling conditions of military industry, she is taking her family back to their home planet, Czerialus. Little does she know Czerialus fares no better under the Empire.

High cranial dome is a Czerialan trait

Comlink with dedicated family frequency

Bronzium necklace, a fourth-generation heirloom

Civilian service rank indicator

WARIA JUNUS

An education regent from Kor Vella, Junus is assigned to investigate the spread of truancy and delinquency among Coronet's youths. A substantial "donation" from the local mayor ensures her reports don't dig too deeply.

MELANAH SAL GRAEFF

Breathmask with built-in comlink

Sienar Fleet Systems development executive Viceprex Sal Graeff routinely visits Corellia to examine her company's factories and speak with government representatives regarding reducing export taxes.

HARRGICK

Atmosphere containment helmet

A blob-like Ugor contained in a humanoid spacesuit, HarrGick had been working at a Ubrikkian factory on Coronet for over a decade. He was laid off when the factory was taken over by the Empire.

GAFFERKY LENZWIN

Filter-weave environment shroud

The pollution levels in Coronet are severe enough to prompt those concerned about their health to leave. Lenzwin, a salesbeing from Hyrotii Assembly Services and a nervous hypochondriac, cannot wait to leave the industrial city. A work assignment brought him here, so he is risking his career by leaving without a sale.

CREV BOMBAASA

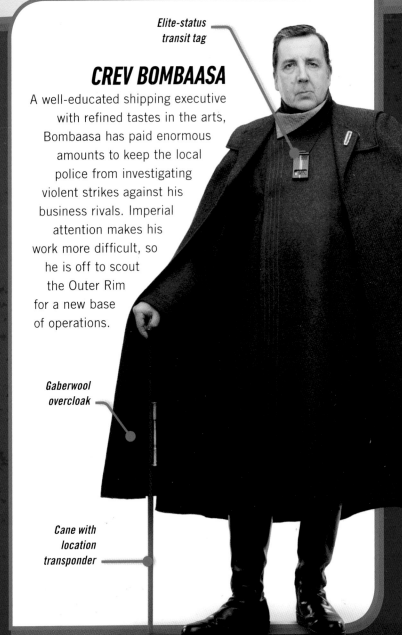

Elite-status transit tag

A well-educated shipping executive with refined tastes in the arts, Bombaasa has paid enormous amounts to keep the local police from investigating violent strikes against his business rivals. Imperial attention makes his work more difficult, so he is off to scout the Outer Rim for a new base of operations.

Gaberwool overcloak

Cane with location transponder

PASHEVIR DUINE

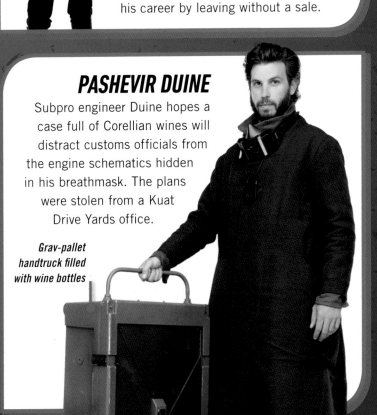

Subpro engineer Duine hopes a case full of Corellian wines will distract customs officials from the engine schematics hidden in his breathmask. The plans were stolen from a Kuat Drive Yards office.

Grav-pallet handtruck filled with wine bottles

CUSTOMS BOOTHS

Weapons scanners and armed guards form a security barrier between most spaceport workers and travellers, but some staff are entirely cocooned in armoured enclosures. Emigration officers process travellers from behind blast-proof transparisteel partitions, with retractable storage drawers used to safely transfer physical objects between parties.

EMIGRATION OFFICERS

On heavily populated worlds, the Empire finds it more efficient to simply induct existing security personnel into the Imperial fold rather than replace them outright with military personnel. Emigration officers are typically locals granted training, equipment and uniforms that allow them to order their neighbours about, in the name of the Empire.

Imperial-issue peaked cap with pin

OFFICER KEELA HEVIS

OFFICER LORU DENHOLT

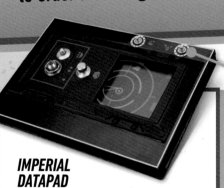

Code key cylinder scomplink port

IMPERIAL DATAPAD

A rugged MerenData IDCA-22 datapad connects emigration officers to the Imperial Enforcement DataCore, which provides information on known criminals and suspects.

ENTRUSTED SECURITY AGENTS

These security agents were attached to CorSec before the rise of the Empire. Still officially part of that local security agency, they are now also considered an asset of the Imperial Security Bureau, with a direct line to that body's Surveillance branch. Typically unarmed, they operate in blast-proof booths with panic buttons that can summon stormtroopers.

L.T.S.O. FALTHINA SHAREST

Lead Transport Security Officer Falthina Sharest's workday has been lengthened repeatedly in the past year due to security demands. This comes with no pay increase. Sharest is looking to balance this inequality by pocketing contraband to resell. Years of experience on the job helps her cover her tracks well. She ensures underlings who have the slightest suspicions about her behaviour are swiftly transferred to another terminal.

> **"YOU COULD BE DETAINED FOR JUST HAVING THIS."**
> – L.T.S.O. FALTHINA SHAREST

Secure comlink line to stormtrooper dispatch

Lipstick shade deliberately flouts Imperial regulations

FIND OUT MORE
The Imperial symbol gives the emigration officer uniform a military feel, but the emigration office is still a civilian agency.

Civilian rank indicator, separate from Imperial military command

Brown tunic a holdover from CorSec livery

DATA FILE
SUBJECT Falthina Sharest
HOMEWORLD Corellia
SPECIES Human
AFFILIATION CorSec
HEIGHT 1.63 m (5 ft 4 in)

33

CHAPTER 2
TRENCH WARFARE

FORCES OF THE EMPIRE

In a show of unprecedented expansion, the Galactic Empire consolidates its power and strengthens its grip on the galaxy. This means venturing further into the lawless reaches of the Outer Rim. The Empire must prepare forces and equipment to deal with both the civilian and criminal resistance it may encounter.

Armour plate and artillery flashback shielding

IMPERIAL ARTILLERY

Heavy armour vehicles are essential for the control of Imperial ground installations. The AT-DT (All Terrain Defence Turret) serves as a piece of mobile battlefield artillery.

MILITARY MIGHT

One of the latest innovations for the Imperial Navy is Sienar Fleet Systems' TIE/rb heavy starfighter (nicknamed the "TIE brute" in some quarters). These starfighters feature heavier armour and firepower than regular TIE fighters. Some fleet admirals are wary of them though, feeling they undercut the strategic importance of larger support ships.

FIND OUT MORE

Inflight support for TIE/rb operations is provided by an MGK-300 integrated droid intelligence. It operates in a manner similar to an astromech counterpart.

Micro-corrugated solar gather panel

Pivoting self-powered SFS H-s9.3 twin laser cannons

DATA FILE

MODEL Sienar Fleet Systems TIE/rb

AFFILIATION Galactic Empire

HEIGHT 10.97 m (36 ft)

LENGTH 8.9 m (29 ft 3 in)

WIDTH 12.2 m (40 ft)

CREW 1

ATMOSPHERIC SPEED 800 kph (500 mph)

WEAPONS Twin laser cannons

Conduit transfers power from solar gather panel to engine systems

Triple-laminate quadranium-reinforced titanium armour

Kerner Optical holographic projector

Ankle joint changes angle when centre foot is deployed

11-3K VIPER DROID

Rotating blaster collar assembly

Articulated manipulator with sampling claws

R5-PHT ASTROMECH DROID

IMPERIAL DROIDS

Tireless droids allow Imperial operations to run at all times, with no need for rest. Droids are programmed with unflagging loyalty to the Empire and constant memory wipes means few droids ever develop anything approaching lifelike personalities. Imperial droids tend to behave like the automatons they are treated as.

E-11 blaster rifle at the ready

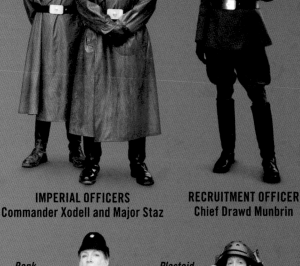

SERVING THE EMPIRE

The growing Empire is enjoying its popularity, particularly in the inner worlds. Recruitment efforts are drawing many young citizens into Imperial military careers. Although Academies offer specialisation in exploration, medicine and merchant services, most cadets are funnelled into the Imperial Navy, Army or Stormtrooper Corps.

STORMTROOPER
TK-5861

IMPERIAL OFFICERS
Commander Xodell and Major Staz

RECRUITMENT OFFICER
Chief Drawd Munbrin

Illuminated traffic wands

Rank plaque

Plastoid blast helmet

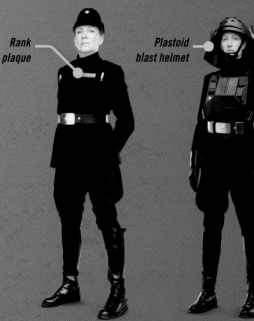

IMPERIAL DECK TECHNICIAN
Specialist Odeffro Msern

IMPERIAL TIE FIGHTER PILOT
Lieutenant Aydn Boship

IMPERIAL FLEET OFFICER
2nd Lieutenant Vell Brank

IMPERIAL ADJUTANT
Warrant Officer Ardwyl Hercho

IMPERIAL FLEET TROOPER
Corporal Zuzanu Latt

FIND OUT MORE
Though the Mimbanese lack heavy artillery, they have improvised mines, tripwires and catapults capable of taking out large vehicles, such as this ill-fated AT-DT.

Haze obscures ruins of former settlements and incoming opposition forces

Insulating mud complicates the detection of friendly and hostile forces on sensors

TRENCH WARFARE

Mimban's dense, ionised atmosphere makes air support difficult, so warfare is largely carried out by entrenched infantry. Imperial combat engineers excavate and fortify trench networks through the thick mud that coats the planet's surface. Command stations are dotted along these trenches, denoted numerically according to position (Station 3–7, for example, is the seventh station in the third trench).

Processing dome for enhanced targeting sensors

WET-WEATHER GEAR

Standard stormtrooper gear has been slightly modified for combat on Mimban. Waterproof capes help keep the mud from caking in armour gaps, and enhanced sensing gear helps cut through the mists in search of body heat signatures.

Capes are known as "slicks" by troopers

MIMBAN

Mimban has been a site of conflict for many decades. Mining interests attracted by deep mineral deposits have long had to contend with natives who understandably object to any intrusive offworlder presence. The Empire has decreed that the mines continue operation nonetheless, and has sent military forces to "pacify" the planet.

Scorch marks
from incoming fire

ORDERS FROM THE TOP

By decree of Grand Moff Tarkin, all regional governors must increase production in the factories, mines and shipyards within their sectors, to help fuel the Imperial war machine. Moff Bin Essada, the regional governor of the Circarpous sector, demands that all resources be stripped from bountiful Mimban. Essada runs this war from the comfort of his offices on the administrative world of Gyndine, far from the mud and chaos.

**ILLUMINATED
TRAFFIC WANDS**

Irradiated sulphur
plasma lights

Signal flares in
stowage loops

Glare shroud

Armoured
transport casing

**NEURO-SAAV TD2.3
ELECTROBINOCULARS**

MILITARY EQUIPMENT

Mimban's temperature, humidity and terrain take a heavy toll on soldiers and their gear. While attempts have been made to weatherproof equipment, the Mimban campaign is run on a very tight budget and such precautions are costly. The shortsightedness of Imperial decision-makers often leads to larger quantities of unreliable supplies, rather than fewer items that do work.

**MICROTHRUST PORTABLE
COM-SCAN RIG**

**INFANTRY SPECIALIST
BACKPACK**

A SCARRED HOMELAND

For most of Mimban's history the planet was ignored by neighbouring worlds, as it was deemed too uncivilised and wild to colonise. Outside influence has recently prompted the harvesting of hyperbaride minerals through dangerous energy mining techniques. As a result, the Mimbanese people have seen their climate ruined, hectares of rainforest cleared and seemingly endless stretches of thick mud spread across the planet.

THE MIMBANESE

One of several intelligent species native to Mimban, but undoubtedly the most aggressive, the Mimbanese are fighting for the very future of their world. These intensely hostile subterranean people climb from the muck to rally against the Imperial presence that has breached the surface of their planet.

Cross strap covers shallow nostrils

Backpack covered in dried sedge grass

Muddy flak jacket

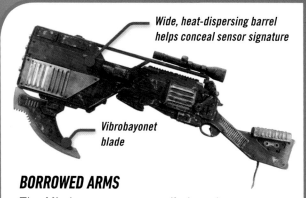

Wide, heat-dispersing barrel helps conceal sensor signature

Vibrobayonet blade

BORROWED ARMS

The Mimbanese were supplied modern weaponry by the Galactic Republic during the Clone Wars. They continue to use the old blasters and vibrobayonets, only retiring them when the weapons finally fall apart.

HIDDEN ENEMY

The Mimbanese have the unsettling ability to disappear in the muck and murk of Mimban, despite their bright red skin and traditional red garments. They adorn themselves with thatch camouflage that conceals them in the sparse underbrush. Their powerful limbs do not tire when pushing through the mud and clay of the battlefield.

PROMISED FREEDOM

Before the Clone Wars, Iasento was the leader of a Mimbanese tribe in the Nanth flatlands. When the planet came to the attention of Separatist invaders, the opposing clone troopers of the 224th Division (the "Mud Jumpers") armed and trained Iasento and his people, promising them freedom when the Separatists were repelled. Iasento now finds himself facing yet another hostile force: the Empire.

Sensor headband with Republic-era infrared and sonar pulse detectors

FIND OUT MORE
The large, unblinking eyes of the Mimbanese have biologically adapted to low light conditions, making them well suited to subterranean life.

Republic-era comms unit

Modified BlasTech F-78 blaster rifle

Woven reed armour

DATA FILE

SUBJECT Iasento

HOMEWORLD Mimban

SPECIES Mimbanese

AFFILIATION Mimbanese Liberation Army

HEIGHT 1.9 m (6 ft 3 in)

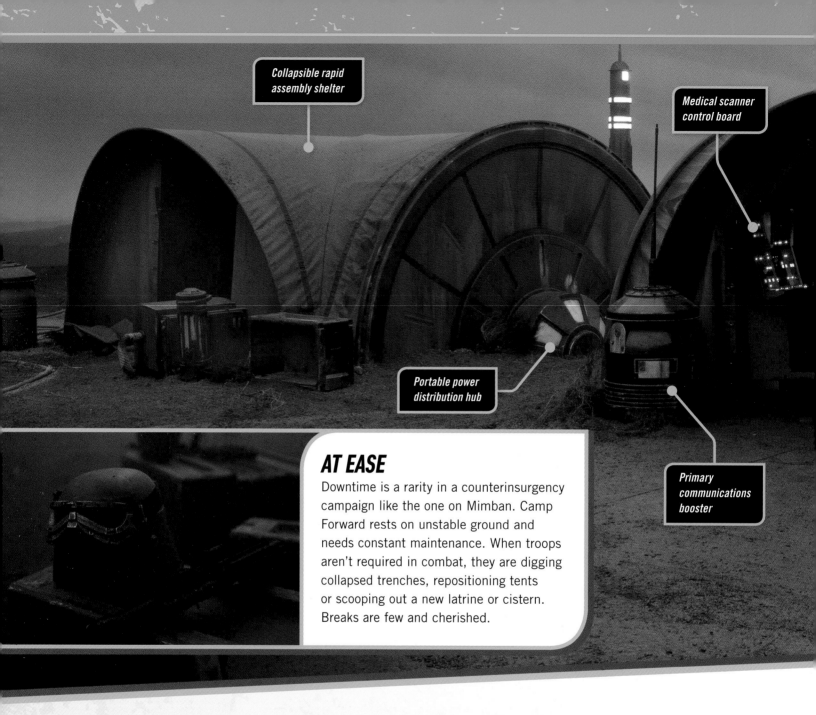

Collapsible rapid
assembly shelter

Medical scanner
control board

Portable power
distribution hub

Primary
communications
booster

AT EASE

Downtime is a rarity in a counterinsurgency campaign like the one on Mimban. Camp Forward rests on unstable ground and needs constant maintenance. When troops aren't required in combat, they are digging collapsed trenches, repositioning tents or scooping out a new latrine or cistern. Breaks are few and cherished.

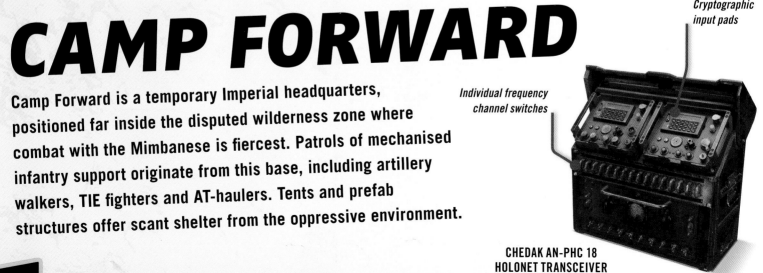

CAMP FORWARD

Camp Forward is a temporary Imperial headquarters, positioned far inside the disputed wilderness zone where combat with the Mimbanese is fiercest. Patrols of mechanised infantry support originate from this base, including artillery walkers, TIE fighters and AT-haulers. Tents and prefab structures offer scant shelter from the oppressive environment.

Cryptographic
input pads

Individual frequency
channel switches

**CHEDAK AN-PHC 18
HOLONET TRANSCEIVER**

TOUGH CONDITIONS

The Mimban swamps create health challenges for the human soldiers stationed there. Prolonged exposure to the mud and standing water leads to such ancient afflictions as "trench foot". During the hot Mimban summers, when atmospheric conditions reach close to human body temperature, soldiers also face dehydration. They can only drink purified imported water, as dangerous microbes are known to infest even vaporator-supplied water. Meanwhile, airborne fungal spores necessitate periodic lung cleanses for troops who neglect to wear their breathmasks.

Irradiator illumination bank helps eliminate mildew

FIND OUT MORE

The IMSUs (Imperial Mobile Surgical Units) are an evolution of a type of prefabricated medcentre deployed in the Clone Wars.

ON THE FRONT LINE

The 224th Imperial Armoured Division is currently slogging it out on Mimban, with conscripted soldiers serving as the latest evolution of the Clone Wars-era Mud Jumpers.

MEDICAL GEAR

Combat medics and their accompanying droids have the latest tools at their disposal, which allow them to patch up wounded soldiers and send them back to the front lines. Though combat conditions are brutal, the weather and terrain are often just as harmful to soldiers.

Reinforced casing

DOUBLE TOOL AND SUPPLY BOX

RUGGEDISED COMBAT MEDIC CASE

Antiseptic field projector

Body support braces

COLLAPSIBLE BATTLEFIELD STRETCHER

MUDTROOPERS

Many soldiers in the Imperial Army were members of local planetary forces who took up arms during the Clone Wars and have since been conscripted into Imperial service. The Imperial Army is gradually being upgraded and replaced with stormtrooper ranks, but for now, regular infantry fight side by side with stormtroopers.

Insolent expression angers superior officers

CORPORAL HAN SOLO

Han Solo has racked up a chequered record in his short time in the Imperial military. Despite showing exceptional piloting skills, Solo was drummed out of the academy for one transgression too far. But rather than waste the money invested in him as a cadet, the Empire transferred him to the infantry to do battle on Mimban instead.

HIGH-IMPACT PLASTOID HELMET

GOGGLES WITH POLARISED LENSES

RESPIRATOR MASK WITH BREATHING TUBES

Mist-cutting chemical glow rod

BLASTECH E-10 BLASTER RIFLE

STANDARD ISSUE

Though the Empire is technologically superior to the tenacious Mimbanese natives, that alone is not enough to secure its victory. Mudtroopers (more formally, Imperial swamp troopers) wear modern partial armour, sealed undersuits, boots to keep moisture out and flared helmets with built-in respirators.

CORPORAL DANITH NODAR

A Carida Academy graduate, Danith Nodar was rotated out of service on the swamp planet Marca for insubordination. She saw transfer to Mimban as punishment and takes out her sour-tempered frustrations on the Mimbanese. Nodar's ferocity in combat unsettles her squadmates but impresses her superiors.

E-22 reciprocating double-barrelled blaster rifle

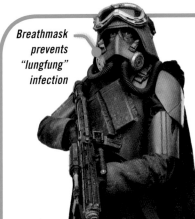

Breathmask prevents "lungfung" infection

PRIVATE COLLUM WOSLO

Woslo was a known brawler in and out of his class in Myomar Academy. His troublemaking tendencies have earned him a series of terrible assignments.

Blaster gas magazine holder

CORPORAL SHARLU GRESLIN

Unable to afford tuition fees to study at Shey Tapani University, Greslin is serving his second tour on Mimban in return for a military scholarship.

CORPORAL WESGER ODRY

An Outer Rim cadet from a world devastated by the Clone Wars, Odry signed up for Imperial service in hopes of seeing the galaxy.

Keeping blaster recoil sleeve mud-free is essential

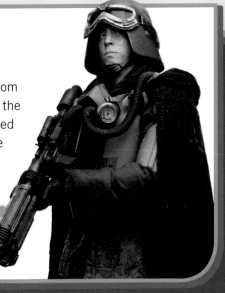

Sandem's medic duty bicep band

SANDEM AND HUMPHREYS

Medic Gorji Sandem rushes into the thick of battle to rescue injured Private Bokret Humphreys and to tend to the younger man's head injuries.

Finders preps pain-relieving gas

Helmet protects Sanwright from physical impact, but doesn't negate concussive force

BATTLEFIELD MEDICS

Specialist Gillen Finders and Sergeant Mattiso Trodu tend to a heavily concussed Corporal Chakobi Sanwright after an explosive assault by Mimbanese guerillas. The 224th Division medics employ arms against the Mimbanese natives without reservation, despite their status as healers. Their harmful behaviour is justified by Imperial interpretations of medical oaths, which dictate they only extend to one's own species. In this case, and almost every other in the Imperial military, that loophole only ensures protection of humans.

UNUSUAL SQUAD

Seemingly out of nowhere, a half-squad of soldiers shows up to take part in a chaotic push against the native insurgents. The newcomers have non-standard weaponry and equipment, raising questions as to both their identities and their motives for entering the fray.

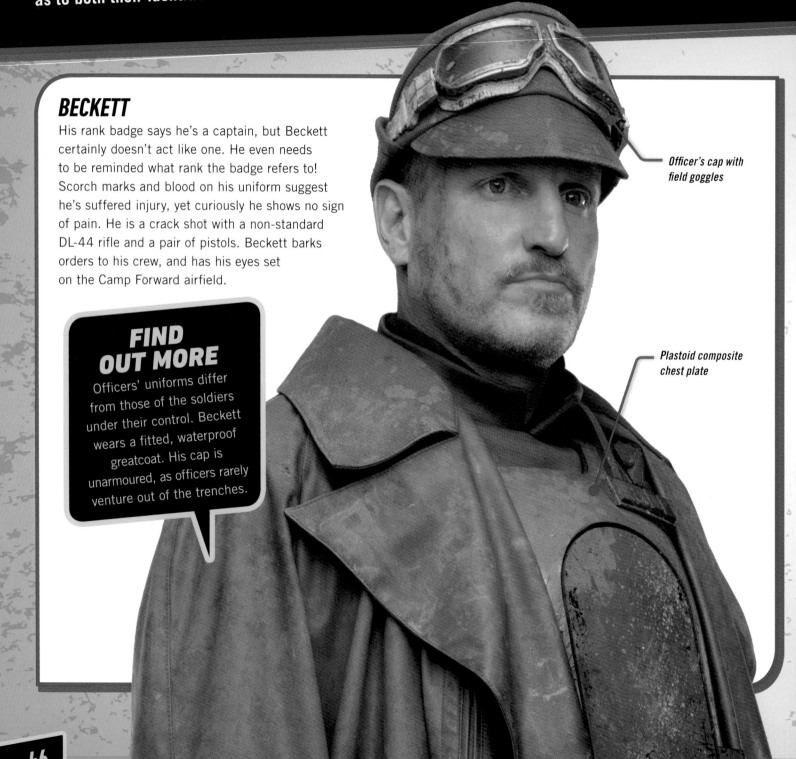

Officer's cap with field goggles

Plastoid composite chest plate

BECKETT

His rank badge says he's a captain, but Beckett certainly doesn't act like one. He even needs to be reminded what rank the badge refers to! Scorch marks and blood on his uniform suggest he's suffered injury, yet curiously he shows no sign of pain. He is a crack shot with a non-standard DL-44 rifle and a pair of pistols. Beckett barks orders to his crew, and has his eyes set on the Camp Forward airfield.

FIND OUT MORE

Officers' uniforms differ from those of the soldiers under their control. Beckett wears a fitted, waterproof greatcoat. His cap is unarmoured, as officers rarely venture out of the trenches.

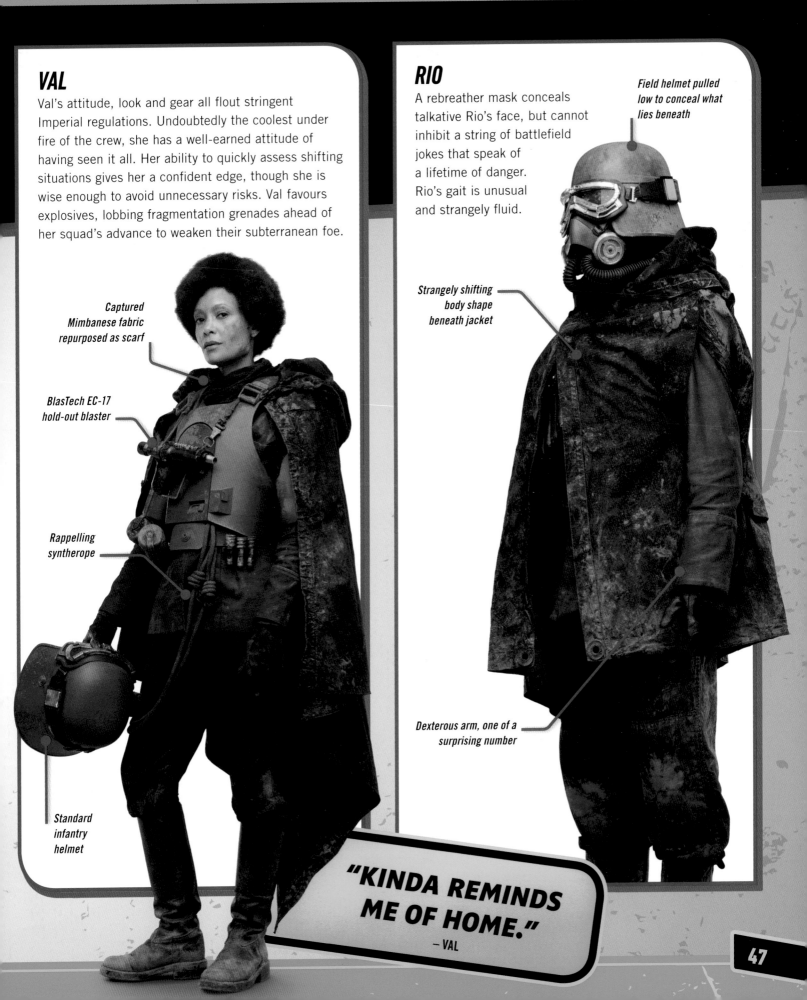

VAL

Val's attitude, look and gear all flout stringent Imperial regulations. Undoubtedly the coolest under fire of the crew, she has a well-earned attitude of having seen it all. Her ability to quickly assess shifting situations gives her a confident edge, though she is wise enough to avoid unnecessary risks. Val favours explosives, lobbing fragmentation grenades ahead of her squad's advance to weaken their subterranean foe.

Captured Mimbanese fabric repurposed as scarf

BlasTech EC-17 hold-out blaster

Rappelling syntherope

Standard infantry helmet

RIO

A rebreather mask conceals talkative Rio's face, but cannot inhibit a string of battlefield jokes that speak of a lifetime of danger. Rio's gait is unusual and strangely fluid.

Field helmet pulled low to conceal what lies beneath

Strangely shifting body shape beneath jacket

Dexterous arm, one of a surprising number

"KINDA REMINDS ME OF HOME."
– VAL

AT-HAULER

The Empire uses AT-haulers for the swift deployment of armoured walker vehicles onto the battlefield. These specialised starships have powerful engines and heavy-duty cargo lifter arms. The haulers are an upgrade from Clone Wars-era carriers, but are now being gradually phased out themselves, in favour of more versatile transports.

FIND OUT MORE
The AT-hauler is strong enough to withstand buckling under heavy loads, thanks to energised tensile strength fields that radiate through the arms.

HEAVY LIFTER
Integral to the AT-hauler are its long propulsion and lifter arms, which use ion engines and linked banks of repulsorlift generators to provide thrust and lift. Magnetic clamps on the underside of the arms lock around the cargo, which can be further secured by localised traction fields, as well as strong, Steelton-manufactured cable ties and winches.

Hardpoint to attach optional sensor, antenna or weapons mount

Arm articulation sliding joint channel

Rotational drum-joint for arm pivot and landing configuration

FLIGHT DECK

A pilot and co-pilot are able to manage both the AT-hauler's flight and cargo-lifting operations. Systems are largely automated, to the extent that the navicomputer contains only a select group of Imperial outposts as pre-calculated hyperspace jump destinations. The Empire also mistakenly believes that this security restriction will deter thieves.

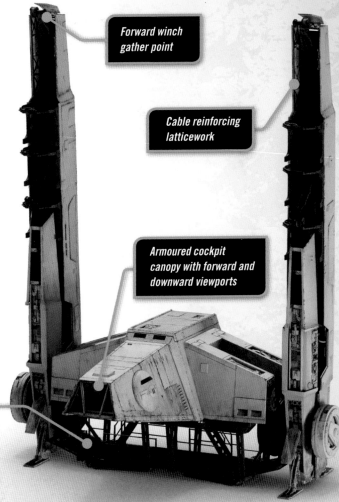

Forward winch gather point

Cable reinforcing latticework

Repulsorlift radiator cell access port

Winching tackle assembly contained within arm

Armoured cockpit canopy with forward and downward viewports

Service gantry and clamp brace platform

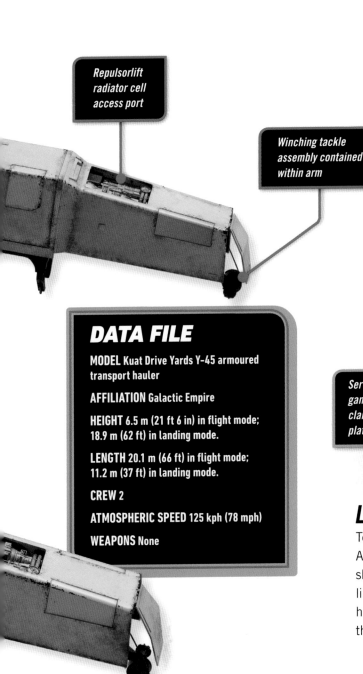

DATA FILE

MODEL Kuat Drive Yards Y-45 armoured transport hauler

AFFILIATION Galactic Empire

HEIGHT 6.5 m (21 ft 6 in) in flight mode; 18.9 m (62 ft) in landing mode.

LENGTH 20.1 m (66 ft) in flight mode; 11.2 m (37 ft) in landing mode.

CREW 2

ATMOSPHERIC SPEED 125 kph (78 mph)

WEAPONS None

LANDING MODE

To save space in hangar bays and landing fields, the AT-hauler rotates its arms when grounded, pointing them skywards. In this way, it is similar to the Empire's favoured line of shuttles from Sienar Fleet Systems, many of which have folding wings. The efficient tensile-field generators in the hauler's arms keep the shuttle hull rigid when landed.

LAIR OF THE BEAST

The commanders of Camp Forward ordered the conversion of an abandoned ammo dump into a makeshift prison for Chewbacca. The shelter's rain tarps have been reallocated elsewhere, leaving the cell full of foul, thick mud. Guards stand watch over the pit, where scraps of food are thrown down to taunt "the Beast" as a form of cruel entertainment.

CHEWBACCA

Wookiees from the forest world of Kashyyyk have been rounded up by the Empire for use as slave labour. Tribes are broken apart as Wookiees are taken to distant star systems, far from their homeworld. Chewie has escaped this fate, but is now a fugitive, looking for his scattered people. In the process, he has once again found himself a prisoner of the Empire.

Forlorn features indicate emotional distress

LOST AND FOUND

Due to his imprisonment, Chewbacca has lost his traditional Wookiee accessories of a bowcaster and bandolier. When he escapes, he soon acquires a scattershot blaster rifle and accompanying ammo harness – both worthy substitutes for now.

— Tool satchels

THE BEAST

Betrayal by a greedy bounty hunter has landed Chewbacca in Imperial custody on Mimban. The local Imperial officers there have neither the resources nor the inclination to process the prisoner and send him back to Kashyyyk. Instead, they keep the filthy, famished Wookiee shackled in a mud-filled pen.

Mud has penetrated deep into his coat

Reinforced plasteel shackle

CHEWIE

At 190 standard years of age, Chewbacca has a distinctly different outlook on life and its priorities than the relative youngsters he finds himself working with. Nonetheless, Chewbacca feels a loyalty to the ragtag group responsible for his freedom, as they have helped him move him a significant step closer to finding his tribe.

DATA FILE
SUBJECT Chewbacca
HOMEWORLD Kashyyyk
SPECIES Wookiee
AFFILIATION Independent
HEIGHT 2.3 m (7 ft 8 in)

> ## "FEED HIM TO THE BEAST."
> – LIEUTENANT BOLANDIN

Ammunition cells crafted by Rio Durant

Merr-Sonn Munitions SX-21 pump-action scatter blaster rifle

FIND OUT MORE
Wookiee fur is often multi-coloured, an evolutionary advantage to help them to blend into the sun-dappled canopies of Kashyyyk's enormous forests.

Shaggy fur conceals surprisingly nimble fingers

CHAPTER 3
THE GREAT ROBBERY

Atmosphere is 99.9 per cent free of modern pollutants

Mount Vastadon, elevation 1,235 metres

COLD CLIMATE

Vandor has a brisk winter that lasts for most of the planet's 435-day year. As the world is largely unsettled and has minimal infrastructure, visitors resort to basic survival techniques to keep warm. Fur is a common clothing material, while local fuel sources include timber and kod'yok dung.

VANDOR

Vandor is a stunning frontier world, marked by jagged snow-capped mountains and lush plains. Even seasoned travellers experience a heady rush when breathing in the remarkably clean air of a world scarcely touched by technology. Vandor is home to the rough-and-tumble trading port of Fort Ypso, as well as a secluded Imperial vault. It is the latter that draws Beckett's crew to the planet.

A TESTING ENVIRONMENT

Vandor's enormous rugged mountains attract thrill-seekers itching to prove their survival skills. Such visitors embark on expeditions with minimal modern tech, leaving behind scraps of fabric when they depart. Not all who set off return to reclaim their token.

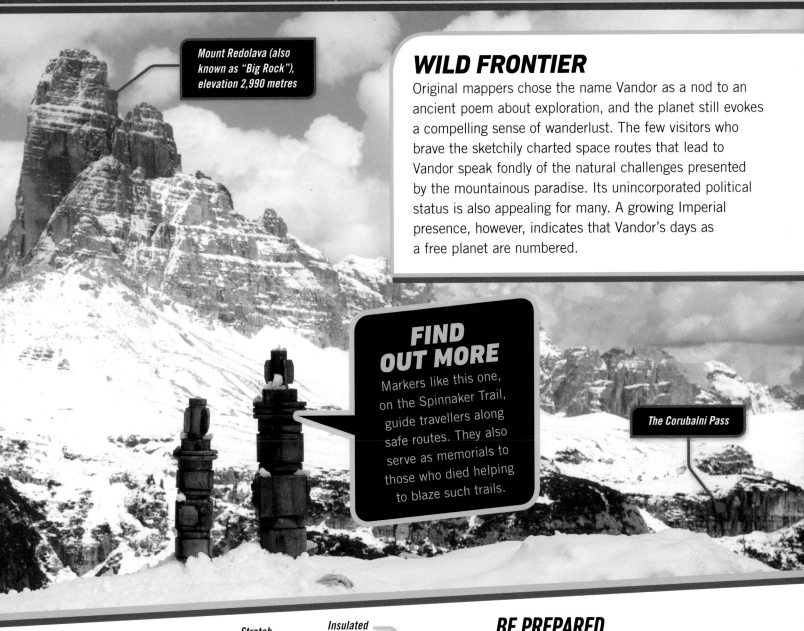

Mount Redolava (also known as "Big Rock"), elevation 2,990 metres

WILD FRONTIER

Original mappers chose the name Vandor as a nod to an ancient poem about exploration, and the planet still evokes a compelling sense of wanderlust. The few visitors who brave the sketchily charted space routes that lead to Vandor speak fondly of the natural challenges presented by the mountainous paradise. Its unincorporated political status is also appealing for many. A growing Imperial presence, however, indicates that Vandor's days as a free planet are numbered.

FIND OUT MORE

Markers like this one, on the Spinnaker Trail, guide travellers along safe routes. They also serve as memorials to those who died helping to blaze such trails.

The Corubalni Pass

Stretch fabric strap

Insulated bottle

BE PREPARED

All modern goods and services are imported to Vandor from off-planet. Survival gear can be purchased at general stores in the few forts and trading camps, but equipment is expensive and in high demand. Most adventurers bring their own tried-and-true equipment, trusting it to keep them alive in the rugged frontier.

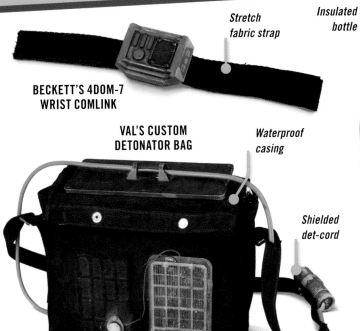

BECKETT'S 4DOM-7 WRIST COMLINK

VAL'S CUSTOM DETONATOR BAG

Waterproof casing

Shielded det-cord

Added drops of Ardennian "Shake-Awake"

RIO'S FLASK

Shatterproof polycarbonate lenses

HAN'S MOUNTAINEERING GOGGLES

Trench created during the Frontier Skirmishes

Metal basket holds tinder in fire pit

AFTER THE SCORE

Beckett's crew pass the time on Vandor discussing hypothetical futures where they have made their fortunes. While Han longs for a starship and Chewbacca simply wishes to find his people, Beckett keeps his goals to himself. It is clear that he has feelings for Val though, and hopes for a peaceful future that the pair can make the most of together.

BECKETT

A grizzled gunslinger from Glee Anselm, Tobias Beckett is a born survivor. He is always quietly working out angles and analysing patterns to ensure he comes out ahead. In order to pay off his debts, Beckett has assembled a team of specialised scoundrels to carry out risky but profitable heists.

Shockproof insulated shell

EYE ON THE TARGET

Using a compact Fabritech 9.5D electromonocular, Beckett seeks out the valuable haul that has drawn him to Vandor. He soon identifies a vulnerable point on the conveyex line serving the Imperial vault.

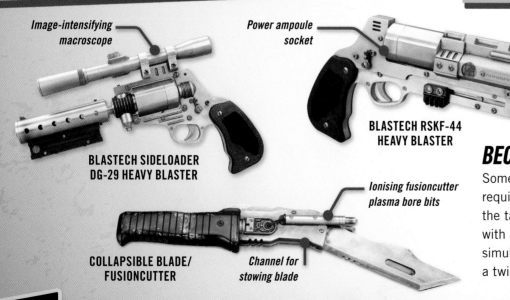

Image-intensifying macroscope

Power ampoule socket

Oxidation marks from heat exposure

BLASTECH SIDELOADER DG-29 HEAVY BLASTER

BLASTECH RSKF-44 HEAVY BLASTER

Ionising fusioncutter plasma bore bits

COLLAPSIBLE BLADE/ FUSIONCUTTER

Channel for stowing blade

BECKETT'S WEAPONS

Sometimes deals fall apart and lethal force is required. Beckett chooses to let his blasters do the talking in these situations. He's a crack shot with both hands and often fires two guns simultaneously. The gunslinger shows off with a twirl of his guns before reholstering them.

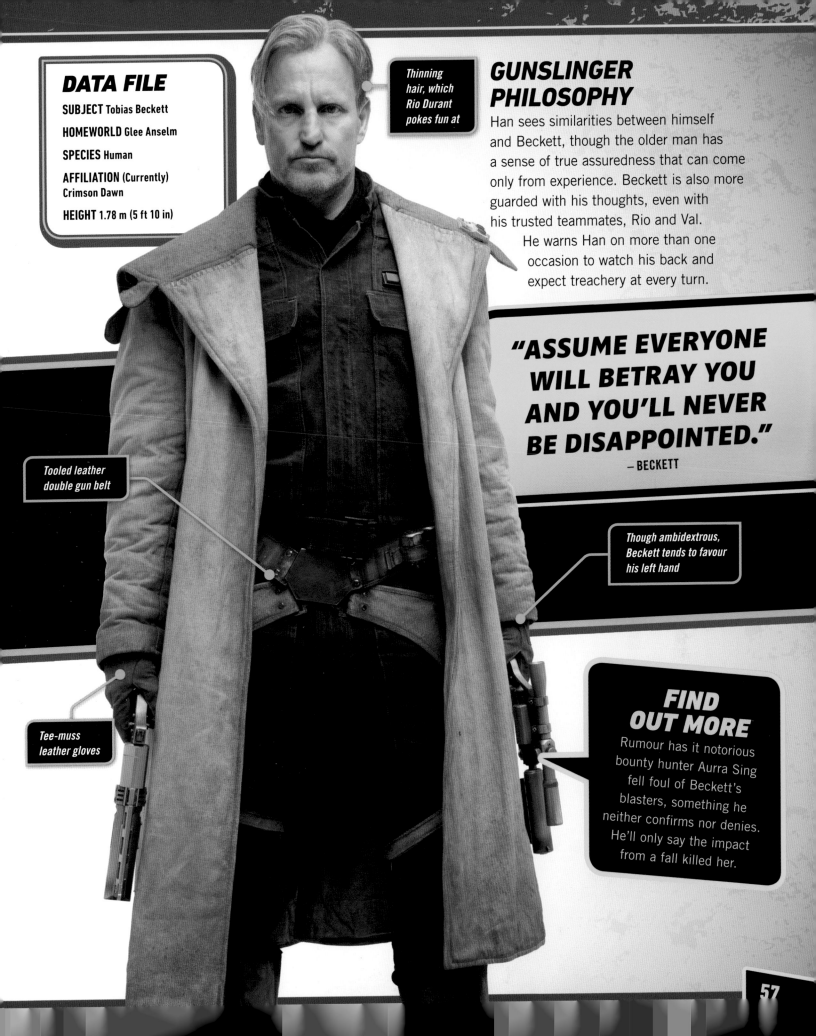

DATA FILE

SUBJECT Tobias Beckett

HOMEWORLD Glee Anselm

SPECIES Human

AFFILIATION (Currently) Crimson Dawn

HEIGHT 1.78 m (5 ft 10 in)

Thinning hair, which Rio Durant pokes fun at

GUNSLINGER PHILOSOPHY

Han sees similarities between himself and Beckett, though the older man has a sense of true assuredness that can come only from experience. Beckett is also more guarded with his thoughts, even with his trusted teammates, Rio and Val. He warns Han on more than one occasion to watch his back and expect treachery at every turn.

"ASSUME EVERYONE WILL BETRAY YOU AND YOU'LL NEVER BE DISAPPOINTED."
— BECKETT

Tooled leather double gun belt

Though ambidextrous, Beckett tends to favour his left hand

Tee-muss leather gloves

FIND OUT MORE
Rumour has it notorious bounty hunter Aurra Sing fell foul of Beckett's blasters, something he neither confirms nor denies. He'll only say the impact from a fall killed her.

OLD SOLDIER

Rio is a veteran of the Freedom's Sons – an independent army that assisted the Republic in the Clone Wars. Joining the army seemed a smart idea for the young Ardennian, but Freedom's Sons never paid a pension. Rio now earns a living applying his military skills to a life of crime.

Military identification tags

RIO DURANT

Rio Durant has carried out dangerous operations alongside Beckett since the early days of their criminal careers. The good-natured Ardennian pilot loves to cook up food for his teammates, as well as help hatch schemes. Rio is up for any challenge, especially if it will make a good story to add to his repertoire of outlandish tales.

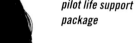

Torplex LVD-41 pilot life support package

Vac-suit sealing ring

Prehensile toes assist Rio in many tasks

THE CREW

Beckett plans to use a stolen Imperial AT-hauler to grab valuable cargo from a conveyex train passing through the Iridium Mountains. To do the job, he needs a squad of professionals. New faces Han Solo and Chewbacca are soon introduced to outlaws Rio Durant and Val, both veterans of Beckett's schemes.

DATA FILE

SUBJECT Rio Durant
HOMEWORLD Ardennia
SPECIES Ardennian
AFFILIATION Beckett's gang
HEIGHT 1.49 m (4 ft 11 in)

Compressed baradium canister

Rocket piton is ready to fire

VAL'S BOMB

Val crafts custom magnetically affixed baradium bombs, a task that requires expert knowledge of chemistry and electronics plus a steady hand. The detonator is keyed to her biological signature.

ADAPTED WEAPON

Val has modified a net-thrower, generally used on Veron to catch gwerax-hai, to become a grapple gun. The device allows her to quickly traverse large distances via a motorised reel of compressed syntherope. The compact set of 12 propellant thrusters inside can launch the piton over 600 metres.

Motorised reel assembly

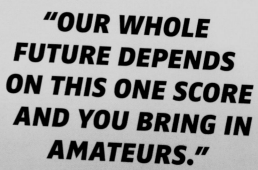

> ## "OUR WHOLE FUTURE DEPENDS ON THIS ONE SCORE AND YOU BRING IN AMATEURS."
> — VAL TO BECKETT

DATA FILE

SUBJECT Val

HOMEWORLD Unknown

SPECIES Human

AFFILIATION Beckett's gang

HEIGHT 1.57 m (5 ft 2 in)

Weather-coated racing goggles ("borrowed" from the Xan sisters)

Mastmot fur lining retains body heat

Sensor-baffling jammer current carried in cable lining

Powered electromag-grip climbing gloves

FIND OUT MORE

Val is an athletic saboteur who can climb, rappel or squeeze into hard-to-reach areas and plant her homemade explosives – with impressively destructive results.

VAL

Val is outwardly expressive and talkative, but she is fiercely guarded about her past. Even her longtime co-conspirators don't know her full name. All the information Beckett has been able to coax from Val is that her father was a musician and she's named after the valachord instrument. The pair share a running joke that Beckett will one day learn to play the instrument in tribute to her.

Abseiling sit harness

CONVEYEX

For rapid transport of special cargo across frontier worlds like Vandor, the Empire uses heavily armoured conveyex vehicles. These long vessels travel along rails winding through treacherous terrain. By not using shuttles or speeders, the Empire is able to maintain tighter security across the cargo's entire journey. Beckett intends to test that security.

Security-locked topside access hatch

Angled walls provide balance as vehicle rocks on tracks

PRECIOUS PAYLOAD

The prized cargo carriage, ICC-5537, carries 400 k-grams of refined coaxium in secure transit canisters. Just one vial of the hypermatter fuel could earn Han a life-changing sum of money.

Illumination bank and data access shroud

Reinforced multi-layered armour hull

Recessed blast door with code-key lock

CARGO CAR

The Imperial Depository on Vandor is specifically built to be hard to reach. Its lack of airfield or hangar facilities prevents direct cargo drops. Standardised containers that would ordinarily fit in the bed of a *Zeta*-class cargo shuttle are instead mounted on the articulated conveyex cradle for delivery.

Hitch joint passive coupler

Magnetic stabiliser pallet

CABIN AND CABOOSE

The conveyex is made up of three main sections. At the front, a drive engine provides the vehicle with its pulling power. This is followed by a series of standardised intermodal cargo containers. Finally, a caboose with stabiliser mount and turret laser cannon brings up the rear of the conveyex.

TWO-TIER TRANSPORT

The conveyex maximises its cargo capacity with a distinctive over/under stacked container configuration. The drive mechanism that pulls the train along a reinforced chain bar is sandwiched between the cargo containers above and below. The whole conveyex sways and bobs as it follows the winding chain through the mountains.

DATA FILE

MODEL Kuat Drive Yards ATD-C45 conveyex engine

AFFILIATION Galactic Empire

HEIGHT 11.28 m (37 ft) entire train; 5.5 m (18 ft) cargo container

LENGTH 230.2 m (755 ft 4 in) entire train; 12.8 m (42 ft) cargo container

CREW 2

SPEED 90 kph (55 mph)

WEAPONS Two medium repeating laser cannons; one double anti-aircraft laser turret

Safety railing

Drive-chain

Shapeshifting data lattice

Stainless steel bead chain

Contact terminals

Drive-link housing drum

Control cabin communications array

IMPERIAL SECURITY

Access to the most secure train cars can only be gained using one-of-a-kind quantum-switch code keys, which are matched to specific biological signatures of their bearers.

FIND OUT MORE

The Empire values security more than scenery, so the conveyex is windowless except for narrow, grilled viewing points above the drive-chain.

COAXIUM

Coaxium is a form of hypermatter – a precious substance that bridges the dimensions of "realspace" and hyperspace. It is an essential fuel for lightspeed travel. A thin coating of coaxium lines a ship's hyperdrive reaction chambers, and when energised allows for transit into the dimension of hyperspace.

OLD AND NEW DISCOVERIES

Refined coaxium is a far cry from the natural form of the substance. Ancient spacefarers discovered coaxium in the organs of purrgil – huge space-travelling creatures. The purrgil inhale space gases containing traces of the gas Clouzon-36, which they metabolise into a hypermatter fuel. This enables them to jump into hyperspace.

DISCOVERY

Using their knowledge of Clouzon-36 gas and purrgil, early explorers were able to work out the kind of conditions that would create natural deposits of coaxium, and where to find them.

MINING

Worlds located near turbulent areas of space often have natural veins of coaxium ore, thanks to the local stellar stresses. An example is Kessel, adjacent to the Maw anomaly.

REFINEMENT

Unrefined coaxium is very volatile, and must be kept as stable as possible. There are limited coaxium refineries, because they require staff with specific technical knowledge.

CONTROL

Refined coaxium is more stable, but it is still shipped under special conditions to prevent theft. The Empire aims to control as many sources of coaxium as possible.

DISTRIBUTION

The Empire uses specialised cargo containers to move large loads of coaxium, but even in such cases it limits the amount kept within a single hold. The Empire uses the fuel across the galaxy, to power its growing fleet.

UNSTABLE IDEA

Reckless Han takes a big risk when he tries to transport unrefined – and highly unstable – coaxium. Transportation of coaxium requires special equipment to prevent the material from being catastrophically jostled. A coaxium explosion is spectacularly violent, tearing at the dimensional barriers that divide the sublight world and hyperspace.

Core racks can be removed separately

Case holds a total of 192 vials

"THAT'S GRADE-A REFINED COAXIUM, WORTH AT LEAST 700 CREDITS."
– HAN TO QI'RA

Balanced carrying handle

Reinforced carbonite storage case

FIND OUT MORE
Tamper-proof datascreen displays internal temperature and kinetic activity, minimising the need to open the case and handle the delicate cargo within.

Core tubes are made out of unreactive metal alloys and glass

MOUNTAIN WATCH

It is hard to maintain visual or technological contact with the conveyex as the vehicle winds its way through the mountains and low clouds. Trackbound sensors provide some data to the Imperial Depository, while 11-3K viper probe droids scout the length of tracks closer to the vault. Responsibility for surveillance and security therefore lies predominantly with the onboard range troopers.

RANGE TROOPERS

The expansion of Imperial territories brings its frontiers to remote outpost worlds, including Vandor. Specialised soldiers known as range stormtroopers defend Imperial interests in such rugged settlements. The range troopers stationed on Vandor are specifically assigned for the protection of the conveyex line.

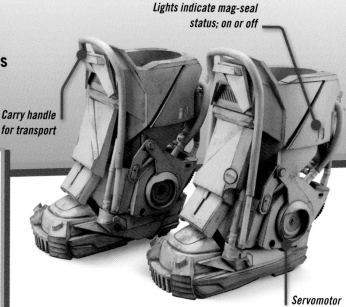

Lights indicate mag-seal status; on or off

Carry handle for transport

Servomotor assembly

Electroscope with enhanced infrared imaging

BLASTER RIFLE

Range troopers carry BlasTech E-10R blaster rifles as their standard weaponry. The E-10R is a more rugged edition than the standard E-11, with enhanced electroscope optics and stabiliser add-ons.

Extended stock with extra ammunition load

GRIPPING GEAR

Range troopers wear heavy duty magnetomic gription boots for conveyex security duty. If a threat presents itself, troopers emerge from their passenger car and inspect the train as it hurls through the mountains at 90 kilometres per hour. While it may seem more prudent to halt the train as they investigate, the Empire's priority is that the conveyex run on time.

FIND OUT MORE

Instead of the delicate miniaturisation found in standard trooper gear, the range trooper helmet features larger, tougher components which are easier to repair by hand.

DATA FILE

SUBJECT Captain Denwade Banevans

HOMEWORLD Carida

SPECIES Human

AFFILIATION Galactic Empire

HEIGHT 1.80 m (5 ft 11 in)

"TRESPASSERS ON THE VEHICLE! FAN OUT AND ELIMINATE!"

— CAPTAIN DENWADE BANEVANS

Waterproof stowage packs for survival gear

Synth-fur lined kama

Vambrace armour with integrated gription boot interface controls

Servomotor brace connection point

PROUD AND TOUGH

Range troopers are some of the hardiest soldiers in the Imperial military, and they pride themselves on operating without support or comforts. They are confident in any environment and are prepared to live off the land, even in the harshest elements. In rare instances where range troopers interact with other branches of the Imperial military, they enjoy intimidating those they view as "softer" amateurs.

CLOUD-RIDERS

High in the Vandor skies circles a pack of marauders known as the Cloud-Riders. Led by Enfys Nest, they are one of the most infamous swoop pirate gangs in the Outer Rim Territories. They use their modified bikes in high-speed strikes, plundering cargo ships and settlements for riches to sell and gear to use.

FIND OUT MORE

Enfys Nest's gang colours are on bold display to distinguish the Cloud-Riders from rival biker groups like the Dark Star Hellions and the Nova Demons.

WATCH THE SKIES

Enfys Nest leads the Cloud-Riders on strikes. The nomadic group travel aboard a carrier ship, the *Aerie*. The ship rarely lands, since the swoop bikes can launch from altitudes of 400 kilometres.

NEST'S RIDE

Detractors and enthusiasts of swoop bikes describe them in the same way: engines with seats. They are crude, overpowered vehicles with little finesse. Controlling a swoop is difficult, requiring timing, instinct and strength. In the Core Worlds, swoop racing has become a spectator sport, while on frontier worlds it remains the mark of outlaw gangs.

Additional rider stirrup

Triple-cluster turbothrust engines with ion-drive booster

Starboard power cell

Accelerator seat with integral traction field

Handlebars with control linkages to steering vanes

Data collection probe

Air scoop contains forward repulsorcoil

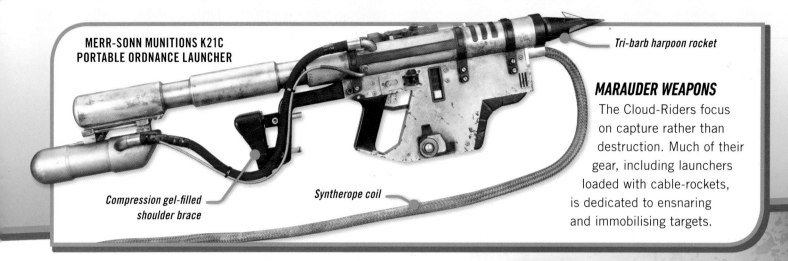

MERR-SONN MUNITIONS K21C PORTABLE ORDNANCE LAUNCHER

Tri-barb harpoon rocket

Compression gel-filled shoulder brace

Syntherope coil

MARAUDER WEAPONS

The Cloud-Riders focus on capture rather than destruction. Much of their gear, including launchers loaded with cable-rockets, is dedicated to ensnaring and immobilising targets.

THE MARAUDERS

The gang's name most accurately describes the "Cloud-Rider" swoop pilots in Nest's gang. Members who leap from sidecars onto target vessels are more accurately called marauders. Baroosh Pawk is a climber and skydiver with more daring than brains. He typically pairs with pilot Tayshin Maxa on raids, riding on her Caelli-Merced Halberd-441.

Traditional Ubese tracking helmet crested with buphasian feathers

Decorative narglatch teeth

Transponder can signal for Cloud-Rider pickup

Reinforced outriggers

Tibanna-jacked DH-17 blaster pistol with vibrobayonet

DATA FILE

MODEL Modified Caelli-Merced Skyblade-330

AFFILIATION Cloud-Riders

HEIGHT 2.94 m (9 ft 8 in)

LENGTH 7.62 m (25 ft)

CREW 1

SPEED 600 kph (375 mph)

Trihedral steering vanes with gang colours on control surfaces

BAROOSH PAWK

Poetry extract reads "Until we reach the last edge, the last opening, the last star, and can go no higher."

Beskar armour plates fan out along articulated servo-joint

HELMET

SHIELD GAUNTLET

A WARRIOR'S WEAPONS

Enfys Nest favours melee weapons over blasters. This has the dual advantage of emphasising Nest's incredible physical skills and unsettling less skilled opponents. Enfys carries a weighted electroripper polearm, tipped with a glowing energy ribbon that crackles with incapacitating voltage and metal-shredding cutting power.

Kinetite charge in base can detonate on impact

ELECTRORIPPER STAFF

ENFYS NEST

Enfys Nest leads the Cloud-Rider swoop gang as it raids and pillages cargo transports on some of the galaxy's toughest planets. Nest's mysterious identity and motives are hidden well beneath substantial armour. All that is known for sure is that the enigmatic marauder poses a serious threat.

Animistic mask design incorporates transmission antennas

Reverse eclipse emblem theorised to be about shining a spotlight in eclipsing darkness

Bantha-fur insulating wrap

Blaster shield extended to protect centre of mass

Repulsorlift boosters increase jump height

WILD FIGHTER

Enfys fights enemies with a relentless ferocity. With powerful weapons and a fleet-footed agility, Enfys can quickly close distances with stunning leaps and deadly swipes. The martial arts at Nest's command are a broad mix of styles that make it difficult to pinpoint the pirate's origins.

MASKED MOTIVES

Reports disagree on the identity, age, gender and even species of the individual behind the Cloud-Rider attacks. Analysis of Nest's strikes give few clues about the being hidden beneath the mask. While Nest's targets seem random at first glance, a careful assessment does show that the Cloud-Riders harbour a particular hostility towards Crimson Dawn operations.

Chromed visor

"ENFYS NEST HAS BEEN A NAGGING IRRITATION FOR FAR TOO LONG."
– DRYDEN VOS

FIND OUT MORE
Vocoder chest box and comlink unit allow contact with the rest of the gang, but also make Enfys' true voice unidentifiable.

DATA FILE

SUBJECT Enfys Nest

HOMEWORLD Unknown

SPECIES Unknown

AFFILIATION Cloud-Riders

HEIGHT 1.67 m (5 ft 5 in)

Insulated grasp length on powered electroripper staff

Wrist-mounted shields fold in for storage

Cape makes it hard to discern body shape for targeting

CHAPTER 4
PLACE YOUR BETS

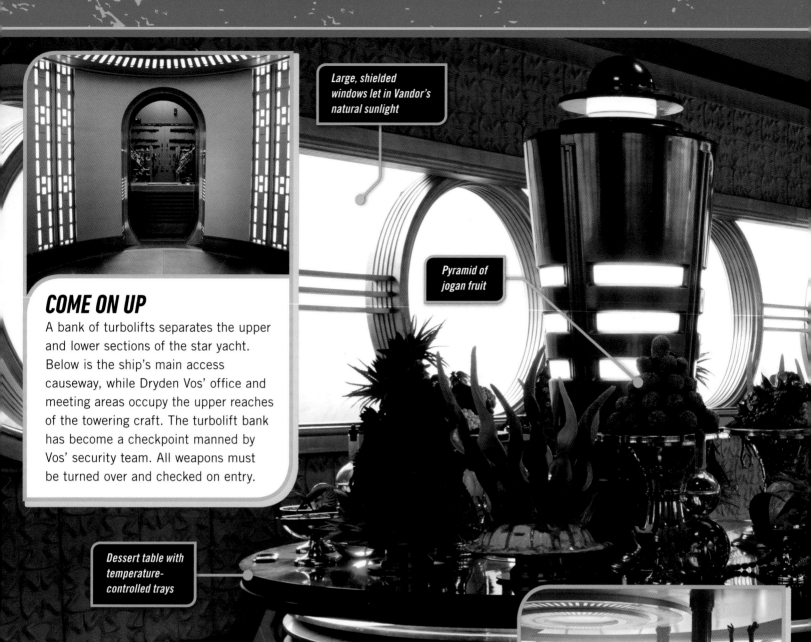

Large, shielded windows let in Vandor's natural sunlight

Pyramid of jogan fruit

COME ON UP

A bank of turbolifts separates the upper and lower sections of the star yacht. Below is the ship's main access causeway, while Dryden Vos' office and meeting areas occupy the upper reaches of the towering craft. The turbolift bank has become a checkpoint manned by Vos' security team. All weapons must be turned over and checked on entry.

Dessert table with temperature-controlled trays

STAR YACHT

Dryden Vos, a senior member of the Crimson Dawn crime syndicate, travels the galaxy in an elegant Kalevalan star yacht named the *First Light*. Currently moored on Vandor, the vessel contains luxurious accommodation on a par with the galaxy's most exclusive hotels or starliners. Vos wishes to show off his taste and sophistication, so spares no expense aboard the yacht.

DIVERTING ACTIVITIES

Visitors to the *First Light* are encouraged to mix business with pleasure. Vos employs master chef Shrindi Meille to create spectacular dishes for guests to graze on, while live music enables more energetic individuals to dance.

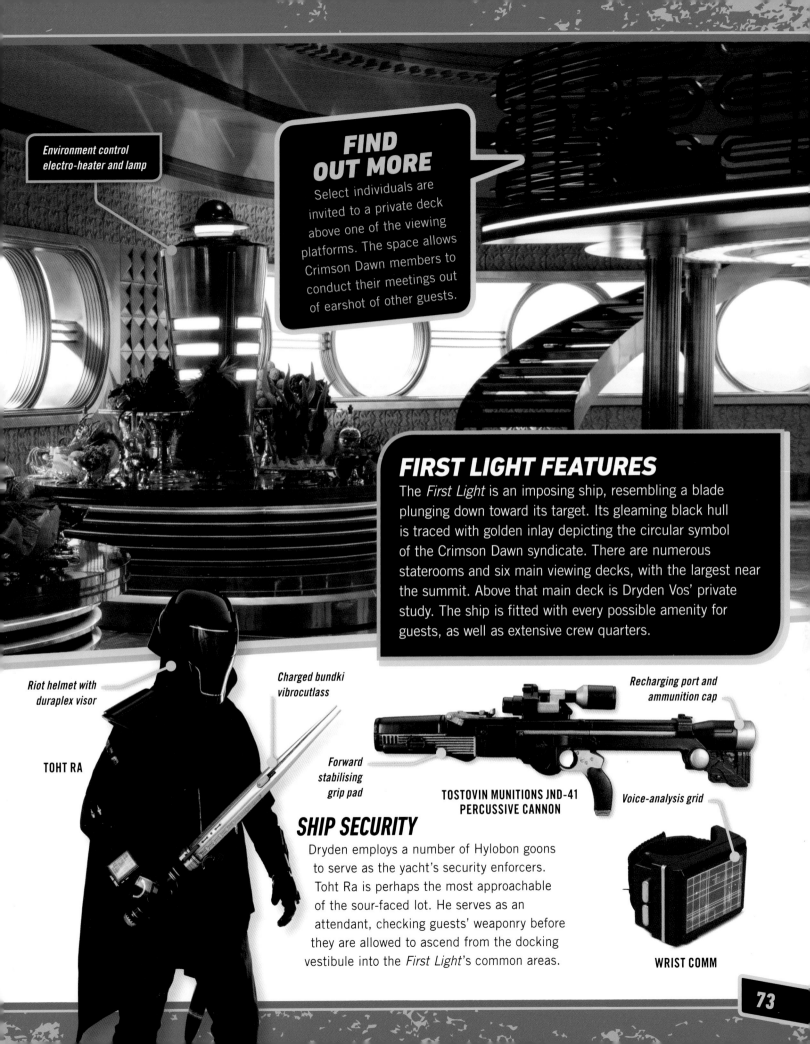

Environment control electro-heater and lamp

FIND OUT MORE

Select individuals are invited to a private deck above one of the viewing platforms. The space allows Crimson Dawn members to conduct their meetings out of earshot of other guests.

FIRST LIGHT FEATURES

The *First Light* is an imposing ship, resembling a blade plunging down toward its target. Its gleaming black hull is traced with golden inlay depicting the circular symbol of the Crimson Dawn syndicate. There are numerous staterooms and six main viewing decks, with the largest near the summit. Above that main deck is Dryden Vos' private study. The ship is fitted with every possible amenity for guests, as well as extensive crew quarters.

Riot helmet with duraplex visor

Charged bundki vibrocutlass

Recharging port and ammunition cap

TOHT RA

Forward stabilising grip pad

TOSTOVIN MUNITIONS JND-41 PERCUSSIVE CANNON

Voice-analysis grid

SHIP SECURITY

Dryden employs a number of Hylobon goons to serve as the yacht's security enforcers. Toht Ra is perhaps the most approachable of the sour-faced lot. He serves as an attendant, checking guests' weaponry before they are allowed to ascend from the docking vestibule into the *First Light*'s common areas.

WRIST COMM

CURIOSITY COLLECTOR

Vos has a passion for antiquities, and his work on behalf of Crimson Dawn has given him the resources to build a one-of-a-kind collection. Those looking to curry favour with Vos – or desperately seeking his forgiveness – present him with lavish gifts. There are no guarantees of appreciation from the temperamental Vos though, however priceless the offering.

Reconstructed Sith holocron that Vos intends to give to a suitable benefactor

DRYDEN VOS

Dryden Vos is the face of an emerging criminal syndicate known as Crimson Dawn. The organisation has quickly established a reputation for ruthlessness, even among the galaxy's crowded criminal underworld. Dryden is no crude cutthroat, however. He takes pride in being seen as a refined gentleman with a taste for luxury. It is unknown if this is from a privileged upbringing. The earliest records of Vos' past is as a merciless enforcer.

Aurodium-cinnabar matrix

FASHION AND FUNCTION

Among Vos' most prized possessions is the signet ring of Crimson Dawn, worn only by the most trusted capos of the shadowy organisation. The ring is encoded to open protected data systems.

SHARP EDGED

Vos wields a matched pair of custom Kyuzo petars. The blades have been designed to fit his humanoid fingers and thumb-claw, and are weighted for his reach and fighting style. The daggers have a sharp, tempered carbon edge, but with a flick of a button, they become lined with a scintillating monomolecular energy cord, further increasing their deadliness.

Bronzium knuckle-guard

Conductive blade edge

Rechargeable power cell (sealed in palm hilt)

SOPHISTICATED VILLAINY

Never one to skulk in shadows, Dryden leads a larger-than-life existence. He socialises with the rich and famous, while cutting deals and throats behind closed doors. He can snap from cultured gentleman to ferocious killer in an instant, and few receive more than a single warning not to fail him.

FIND OUT MORE

A head wound is evidence of recent trauma. The incision has been mechnostapled by Dryden's on-staff physician.

Striation linked to circulatory system activity and adrenaline levels

Baffleweave cape is difficult for weapons scanners to penetrate

> "TEST MY PATIENCE FOR EVEN ONE SECOND AND SEE WHAT HAPPENS."
> — DRYDEN VOS

Coded datapad and financial tracker

Custom handmade Pantora-silk suit

DATA FILE

SUBJECT Dryden Vos

HOMEWORLD Unknown

SPECIES Near-human

AFFILIATION Crimson Dawn

HEIGHT 1.92 m (6 ft 3 in)

Wrist-comm and biorhythm reader

FIRST LIGHT STAFF

The staff of the *First Light* sign on for a life of perpetual travel, with scattered ports of call wherever Dryden Vos' duties and desires take the massive yacht. Intrigues and relationships – some friendly, others decidedly not – flourish in such close quarters.

AEMON GREMM

The captain of Dyrden Vos' security forces, Aemon Gremm is the only enforcer with a direct line to Vos himself. He insists all security concerns funnel through him. In this way, he makes himself an essential part of Dryden's operation and takes all the credit for his security staff's work. Physical domination is a very strong social trait among Hylobons, which is why Vos employs the species as enforcers.

GL-OT15

The *First Light* employs vendor droids as attendants, capitalising on their preprogrammed obsequiousness and desire to make customers happy. GL-OT15 operates the principal turbolift that brings guests from the docking entrance to the lofty lounge and office decks. GL-OT15 also has a bank of weapon scanners.

Close-range sensor modules can detect energy and chemical weaponry

Scar is a souvenir of a violent past

Segmented riot helmet, open configuration

PA-LT4

Fresh fruit assortment

One of a team of server droids trying to remain inconspicuous and avoid getting underfoot, PA-LT4 is a polished A-LT utility unit topped with a temperature-controlled serving tray.

Precision-engineered traction treads

AURODIA VENTAFOLI

Multi-vocoder boosts her voice to non-human frequencies

Corded auropyle dress

A bestselling recording artist billed as "Chanteuse of the Stars", Aurodia Ventafoli is in high demand. Touring makes it rare for her to settle in one place for too long, but Dryden Vos offered a hefty sum to book her for an extended residency on the yacht. He pairs her with a classic supper-club singer.

LULEO PRIMOC

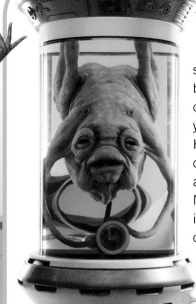

First impressions of this tiny Gallusian might not suggest a recording legend, but Luleo Primoc was a chart-topping singer in the years before the Clone Wars. He also starred in a series of old holomovies while wearing a dashing humanoid exo-suit. Now past his prime, Luleo is still favoured by retro-collectors and enthusiasts.

Repulsorlift-fitted flask filled with formaldehyde

MARGO

Margo, an Imroosian who hails from a volcanic planet, is Dryden Vos' concierge and handles all guest amenities aboard the *First Light*. Margo's people have evolved a flinty, chalk-like skin to resist the searing temperatures of their home. Personally, Margo detested that environment, and she revels in the cool interior of the yacht.

Ottegan charbake smelt necklace

Shimmersilk gown

OTTILIE

Ottilie is a chic server entrusted to attend to Dryden's personal guests. Efficient and observant, she shows just enough initiative to work independently, but not enough to worry her bosses.

Tray of quanya reserve intended for Count Chrodber of Serenno

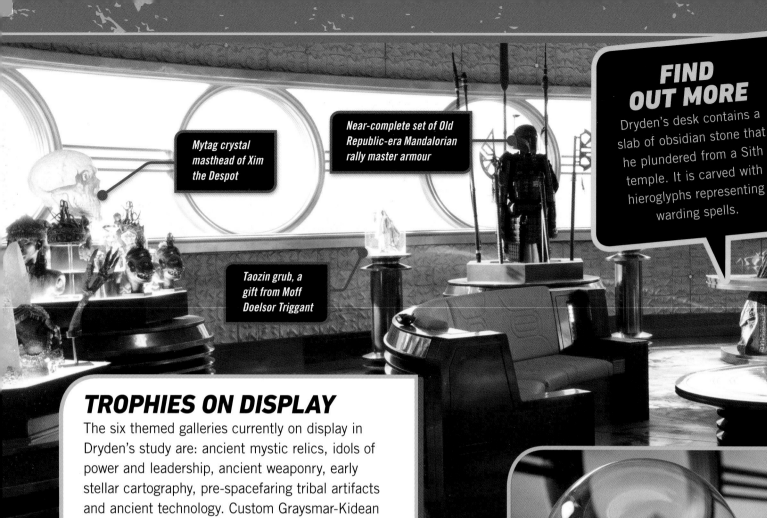

Mytag crystal masthead of Xim the Despot

Near-complete set of Old Republic-era Mandalorian rally master armour

FIND OUT MORE
Dryden's desk contains a slab of obsidian stone that he plundered from a Sith temple. It is carved with hieroglyphs representing warding spells.

Taozin grub, a gift from Moff Doelsor Triggant

TROPHIES ON DISPLAY

The six themed galleries currently on display in Dryden's study are: ancient mystic relics, idols of power and leadership, ancient weaponry, early stellar cartography, pre-spacefaring tribal artifacts and ancient technology. Custom Graysmar-Kidean units create invisible preservation fields around the objects, maintaining specific humidity, pressure and temperature requirements to keep any ancient or fragile pieces in pristine condition.

DRYDEN'S STUDY

Located near the summit of his towering star yacht is Dryden's spacious study. Wrap-around windows provide stunning views of the ship's surroundings. However, the real spectacle is Vos' meticulously curated personal museum of rare treasures: carefully arranged displays that contain just a small selection of his trophies.

PRESERVED MENAGERIE

Rare animals – including a Tran Mariel runyip – are kept in suspended animation within sealed jars. The jars sit upon entropy field-generating pedestals, which preserve the priceless contents.

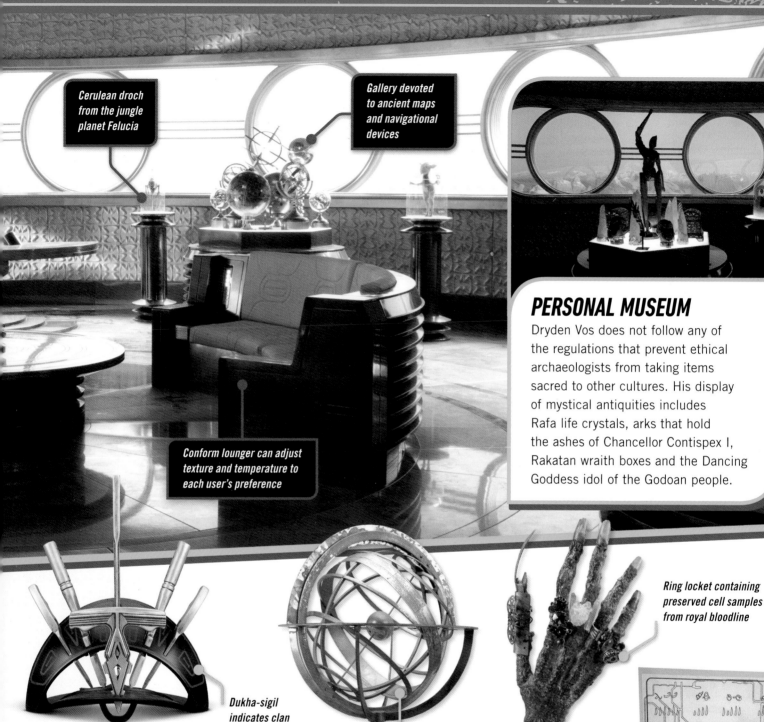

Cerulean droch from the jungle planet Felucia

Gallery devoted to ancient maps and navigational devices

Conform lounger can adjust texture and temperature to each user's preference

PERSONAL MUSEUM

Dryden Vos does not follow any of the regulations that prevent ethical archaeologists from taking items sacred to other cultures. His display of mystical antiquities includes Rafa life crystals, arks that hold the ashes of Chancellor Contispex I, Rakatan wraith boxes and the Dancing Goddess idol of the Godoan people.

TRADITIONAL NOGHRI CARVER SET

Dukha-sigil indicates clan allegiance

OBJECTS OF INTEREST

The displays in Dryden's study are only a fraction of the rarities in his collection. Vos rotates out the galleries at whim, requesting items from storehouses on Tanaab, Byblos, Cato Neimoidia and elsewhere. He employs well-paid buyers and relic-hunters to risk their lives in order to find him new trophies.

Band tracks progression of constellations through the sky

ALDERAANIAN ARMILLARY SPHERE

Ring locket containing preserved cell samples from royal bloodline

MUMMIFIED HAND OF THE LOST KING OF DURO

Glyphs allegedly pinpoint the long-lost Queen of Ranroon ship

ANCIENT NAVI COMPUTER DATAPLAQUE

PARTY GUESTS

Dryden's yacht attracts frivolous thrill-seekers who flock to the rich and powerful guests with dreams of catching residual fame. Most are apolitical and amoral: whether or not they know about Dryden Vos' criminal activities is inconsequential. The party must go on.

Parabolic headdress and masquerade mask

Metachromatic trevalla cloth

DAMICI STALADO

A social chameleon who believes physical shape to be arbitrary, Stalado is in the midst of deep-tissue regrafting and splice therapy to transform her features once again.

BLYSTO NOXTON

Noxton is an avant-garde holovid artist who fancies himself a deep thinker. His partygoing is research (as he puts it) for a masterpiece work of holocinema yet to come.

Fineweave sherculién-cloth

Magnetic amulet he mistakenly believes focuses his thoughts

Quadnocular vision – a Dyplotid trait – allows sight in infrared and ultraviolet spectrum

Formal yet understated business wear

TARUBO BUNZO

Bunzo is an Astantu Distillery sales representative from the Ring of Kafrene. He brings samples of his finest reserves in hopes of landing a lucrative business deal with Dryden Vos.

Recumbent crest, common to Nithorn males

Keratin beak

HIRANG BIRREN

A cruise ship talent scout with a keen ear for music, Birren has been unwittingly singing along with the yacht's entertainment in his own guttural birdsong.

Ear includes organic mid-cochlear recording device

Flask of Vandor ice water to keep her focused

KARA SAFWAN

Kara Safwan is a spy hired by the rival Rang Clan to gather intel on Crimson Dawn operations. Though Safwan blends in well with the revellers, Margo suspects she is up to something and has been discreetly blocking her attempts to get deeper into Dryden Vos' inner circle.

Metallic hemidroxl fabric

SABLIX VEEN

Veen is a fashion designer and model hoping to boost her career by being seen at one of Dryden's parties.

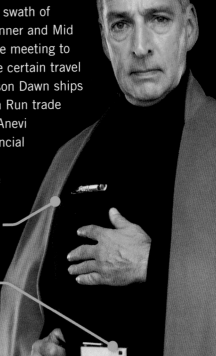

DILES ANEVI

Diles Anevi is Governor of the Expansion Region, a swath of space between the Inner and Mid Rims. He and Vos are meeting to strike a deal to waive certain travel restrictions on Crimson Dawn ships using the Great Gran Run trade route. In exchange, Anevi hopes to secure financial contributions to charitable causes he cares dearly about.

Gaberwool mantle of office

Buckle contains transactional credit chip portfolio

Faux-cones on male headdress are a playful choice

HADO GWIN AND BOSHTI ANILEE

Dancers Hado and Boshti are a Twi'lek couple who follow the *First Light* from port to port. The pair trained for a year at the famous Dette Lawnic Dance Academy on Alderaan before joining the competitive circuit. They are now trophy winners in three sectors.

QI'RA ON THE RISE

When Qi'ra was a child, her cautious nature helped her succeed among the scrumrats. This quality is now teamed with a mature, strategic mind that allows her to navigate the far more dangerous waters of Crimson Dawn operations. She hides her true desires and intentions, using charm and wit to deflect probing questions from Dryden Vos. This cool, calculating front will take some getting used to for her old friend Han.

QI'RA

Qi'ra has put her life as a powerless street urchin behind her, and has managed to move up in rank and reputation within Crimson Dawn. Dryden Vos has taken a close interest in her and she now serves as the volatile gangster's most trusted lieutenant.

Crimson Dawn half-logo bib necklace

Black clothing coordinates with that of other gang members

Onyxian belt with gold striping

EXPLOSIVES CASE

Through Crimson Dawn contacts, Qi'ra has access to whatever tools a plan requires. The 24 grenades in this reinforced case have charges including explosive, smoke and sedative gas.

Shock-absorbing gel layer keeps explosives from rattling in transit

DRESSED FOR SUCCESS

Qi'ra's wardrobe consists of smart, tailored outfits from the galaxy's leading designers – a far cry from the tattered clothes she wore on Corellia. Qi'ra looks right at home negotiating trade deals with magnates who are unaware of her humble origins. The clothes are also designed so that, when necessary, they do not hinder her expert martial arts skills.

DATA FILE

SUBJECT Qi'ra

HOMEWORLD Corellia

SPECIES Human

AFFILIATION Crimson Dawn; formerly White Worms

HEIGHT 1.58 m (5 ft 2 in)

UPPER MANAGEMENT

With a staff of servants to instruct as she sees fit, Qi'ra manages Dryden Vos' schedule, serves as his strategist and advisor and carefully monitors the meetings he takes aboard his yacht. Dryden trusts her with his business, and is grooming her to be his eyes and ears on assignments he cannot take on. Unobservant guests assume she is merely a social director and nothing more, unaware of the influence she holds.

Water-sealed moof leather jacket

Voorpak-fur lining provides warmth on trips outside the yacht

Low-slung holster with loops for ammunition

FIND OUT MORE

Qi'ra carries a lightweight Monlitzer S-195 double-barrelled blaster pistol. Its hinged assembly enables the simple loading of reactant gas capsules and power plugs.

"IT'S WHAT WE LEARNED ON THE STREET, HAN; SOMEBODY FALLS, YOU KEEP RUNNING. IT'S HOW YOU STAY ALIVE."

– QI'RA

Mixology computer flags possible side effects of drinks for each species

Bar carved from Vandor resin tree

THE LODGE

Jutting out from the side of a snow-dusted mountain, the Lodge is a Fort Ypso landmark. It is the starting point for many ill-advised adventures into the Vandor wilderness. Triumphant travellers return here to celebrate their conquest of the wilds, while the less successful gather to mourn their losses and plan their next attempt.

SIMPLE PLEASURES

Elaborate distractions are a rarity in rustic Fort Ypso, where harsh environmental conditions put a focus on simply surviving. A keybed in the saloon's corner provides music for the bar. A back room with balcony allows spectators to play and watch sabacc games, while brutal droid fights appeal to more primitive instincts.

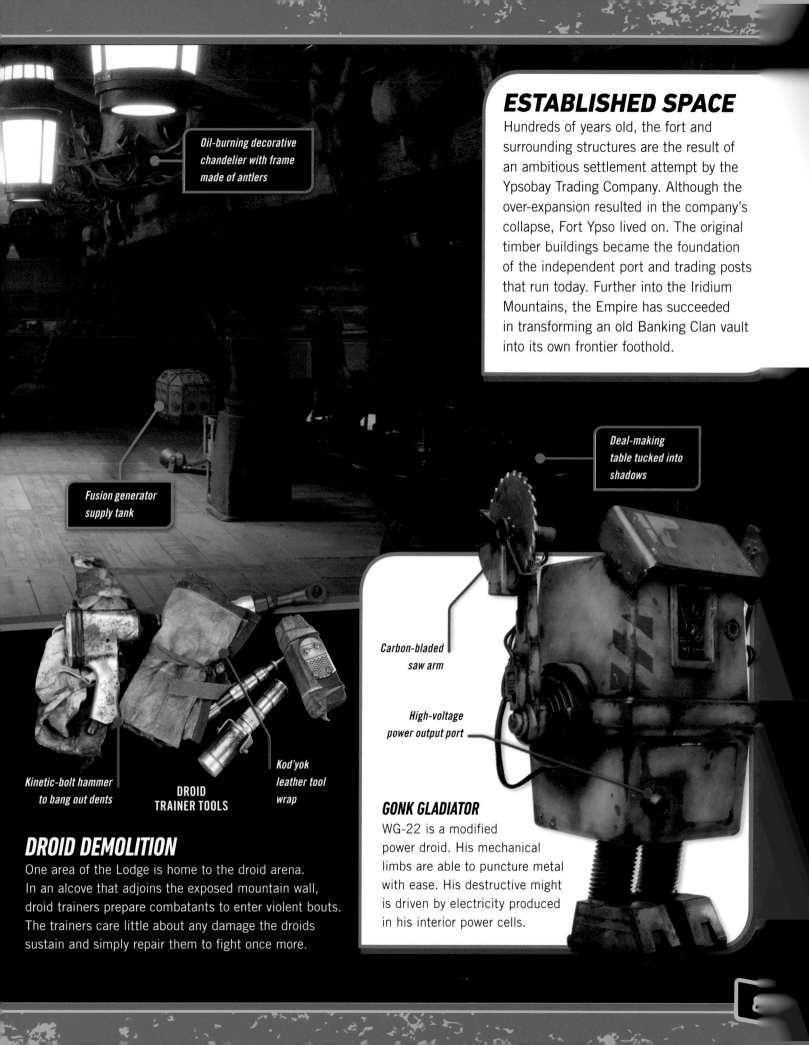

Oil-burning decorative chandelier with frame made of antlers

ESTABLISHED SPACE

Hundreds of years old, the fort and surrounding structures are the result of an ambitious settlement attempt by the Ypsobay Trading Company. Although the over-expansion resulted in the company's collapse, Fort Ypso lived on. The original timber buildings became the foundation of the independent port and trading posts that run today. Further into the Iridium Mountains, the Empire has succeeded in transforming an old Banking Clan vault into its own frontier foothold.

Fusion generator supply tank

Deal-making table tucked into shadows

Carbon-bladed saw arm

High-voltage power output port

Kinetic-bolt hammer to bang out dents

DROID TRAINER TOOLS

Kod'yok leather tool wrap

GONK GLADIATOR

WG-22 is a modified power droid. His mechanical limbs are able to puncture metal with ease. His destructive might is driven by electricity produced in his interior power cells.

DROID DEMOLITION

One area of the Lodge is home to the droid arena. In an alcove that adjoins the exposed mountain wall, droid trainers prepare combatants to enter violent bouts. The trainers care little about any damage the droids sustain and simply repair them to fight once more.

LODGE PATRONS

Many visitors to the Lodge find themselves at a literal and figurative crossroads, with a spaceport and impound lot just down the mountain path. The Lodge provides daring and desperate travellers with a dangerous mix of business and pleasure.

Stylised depiction of a hyperspace simu-tunnel

NALEY FRIFA

Multi-talented Frifa is rarely short of work. As an outlaw tech, she makes illegal modifications or repairs to starships and equipment. She is also a skilled tattoo artist, adept at inking both gang symbols and data-carrying electro-tattoos.

Climber's mask with oxygen concentrators

IOTHENE JACONTRO

Big-game hunter Jacontro is part of a crew who are convinced Vandor's mountains conceal a living vastadon. Despite losing an arm to gangrene after exposure to the elements, this Kerestian trapper returns to Vandor each year. He is willing to brave the wilderness for what many at the Lodge regard as a fool's quest.

RALAKILI

A loathsome rascal who runs the droid fighting pits in the Lodge, Ralakili has hated droids since his planet was ravaged by General Grievous during the Clone Wars.

"Owner" units can remotely give droids a zap of electronic pain

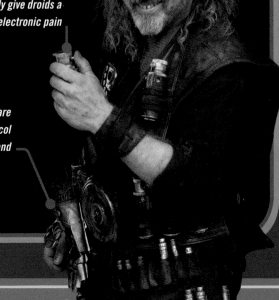

Spare protocol droid hand

"Owner" units are linked to restraining bolts on droids

SANSIZIA CHREET

Chreet is a trainer in the underground droid fighting circuit and an adept codebreaker. She is hired to bypass safety protocols on droids and turn the machines into unwitting assassins.

FUGAS FANDITA

Fandita is an iridium miner employed by the galactic Mining Guild. His mole-like Gotarite heritage makes him well suited for working long hours in low light conditions. He and his coworker spend their time off in the Lodge's bar.

Mighty incisors

Insulated and electro-grounded work coveralls

Cup of imitation juri-juice

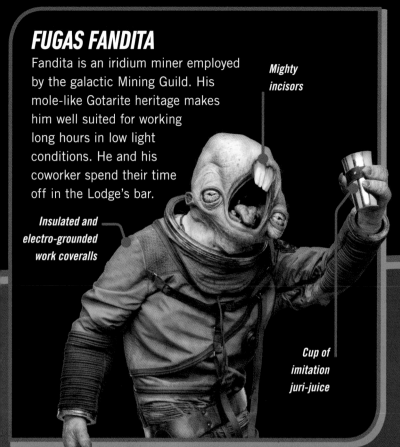

TREGGA

Tregga is a chak-root smuggler from Oslumpex V, who claims to have an innate sense for profitable deals. The sensation is really a side-effect of a malfunctioning brain implant.

Portable translatacomp

Ikopi-skin outfit

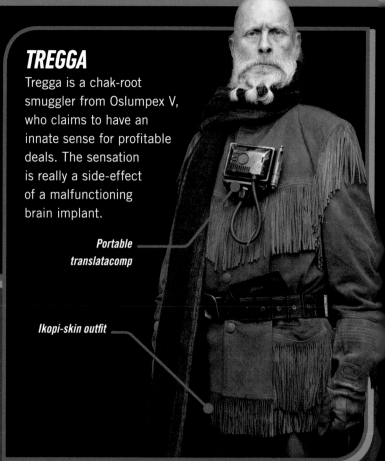

ASTRID FENRIS

Mandalorian-style bob haircut

Synth-hide capelet with concealed pockets

A smuggler from Yir Tangee, Fenris pilots a modified YT-2400 freighter called the *Silver Howl*. Her current scam involves exporting relatively worthless Vandor ice and passing it off as expensive R'alla mineral water. She sells it to gullible customers who believe in the water's promised rejuvenating effects. Astrid insists this is only a short-term scheme to help her settle some debts.

Prax Arms Ophidiax-350 heavy blaster pistol

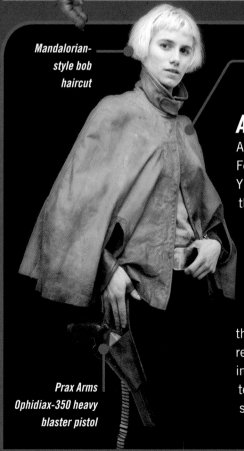

TORDICH ENVLO

Shivering Envlo is a mechanic aboard an independent freighter who hopes his captain finds work on a warmer planet soon. For now, this near-human has engulfed his body in a dense kod'yok fur coat.

Emergency vac-suit provides some insulation

Jacket purchased locally at great cost

Hermetically sealed reactor gloves

Crosh-leather shoes

LANDO CALRISSIAN

Captain Lando Calrissian insists he plans to retire from smuggling and become a full-time gambler instead, shuffling from card game to card game across the galaxy as a professional "sportsman". But with double-talking Lando, this may just be a clever bluff to heighten demand for his services.

Synthetic nanosilk capelet

Ottegan fibrion scarf

Chromium mined from one of Naboo's moons

SLEEK WEAPON

Lando can ably defend himself with a blaster, but he prefers finding non-violent solutions. If he must draw a weapon, it is always a stylish one. His BlasTech SE-14r is plated in brushed chromium, with a Tibrin mother-of-pearl handle.

COOL CUSTOMER

Smooth, sophisticated smuggler Calrissian has been known to slip past the Empire many times. His skills as a schemer, storyteller and con artist are what allow him to avoid trouble and the need to resort to any physical exertion. This means practicality is of little concern when he chooses an outfit.

CALRISSIAN CHRONICLES

Lando is enjoying some downtime after a hair-raising smuggling run from Felucia, which helped him pay off his debts. He is using the time to record the *Calrissian Chronicles*, a self-narrated account of his colourful escapades. So far, he's recounted (and exaggerated) his adventures in the Rafa system and a caper involving the Mindharp of Sharu. Calrissian estimates that he's got at least a trilogy in him, but he'll see how the first one sells.

DATA FILE

SUBJECT Lando Calrissian

HOMEWORLD Socorro

SPECIES Human

AFFILIATION Independent

HEIGHT 1.74 m (5 ft 8.5 in)

"EVERYTHING YOU'VE HEARD ABOUT ME IS TRUE."
– LANDO CALRISSIAN

Winning smile

FIND OUT MORE

Lando holds a winning hand of sabacc, using Numidian Prime rules. He has studied more than 80 variant forms of sabacc, and knows how to cheat in all of them.

Beckon call transponder chit

Bespoke cape from tailor on a subtropical moon in the Oseon belt

Sleeve hides green sylop card as a bit of sabacc insurance

SABACC

Perhaps the oldest and most popular card game in the galaxy, sabacc has spawned a huge number of variations, all with different rules. Common traits include an emphasis on bluffing, betting and raising stakes. An element of chance is also common, meaning card totals – and therefore fortunes – may shift in the blink of an eye.

PULL UP A SEAT
In the back room of the Lodge, there is always a sabacc game in progress. When stakes are high, an eager crowd gathers to watch the game unfold.

Dried chak-root used as gambling stake

Beverage cup filled by a floating repurposed bacta-administering nurse droid

100-credit Imperial coin

Sabacc deck holder crafted to hold exactly 62 cards

Sabacc dealer token

Crystalline vertex coin

Mandalorian coinage

Chance cubes for Corellian Spike rules

"Honest stones" change colour in the presence of many electronic cheating devices

AN UNPREDICTABLE GAME
The object of Corellian Spike sabacc is to achieve a card total closest to zero. Two pots accumulate in value during a game, with the hand pot won each round. The sabacc pot grows larger as the game progresses and is won by the player who draws a total of exactly zero, ending the game. Players bet based on their confidence in their hand. After each betting phase, the spike dice are rolled. A roll of doubles discards each player's hand and replaces it with unseen cards from the deck – potentially improving or destroying a player's chances.

Card has a value of positive one

THE CARDS
Corellian Spike rules favour a 62-card deck, with cards ranging in value from –10 to 10, and two zero-value cards known as sylops (Old Corellian for "idiots").

LODGE PLAYERS

Nerf-leather overcoat

SIX EYES

Argus "Six Eyes" Panox has some clear advantages when playing cards. His six flexible eyestalks are characteristic of his Azumel heritage. They are also responsible for his nickname and reputation for peeking at other players' hands. Thoughtful Six Eyes literally chews his cud as he keeps an eye on the competition.

Electrosensitive antennae

THE TWINS

Their nickname is misleading, as Lark and Jonk are not twins, but rather a single entity with two heads – the norm in the Danzikan species. House rules state they must play as a single player. Otherwise they would be suspected of tactically driving up the pot and then splitting the winnings.

Oiled headwrap keeps scales from drying out

KARJJ

Bad luck sticks to Karjj. He has a troubled marriage, a clunker of a ship and crushing debts. It's his foul-tempered, distracted state that makes him a welcome addition to a sabacc table. He can be counted on to lose his money as quickly as he loses his temper.

Atmosphere exchange breathing tubes

BIG GUY

The Octeroid smuggler Glaucus is known alternately as "Big Guy" and "Big Eye", although his loose grasp of Basic means he doesn't notice the difference. He prefers to watch rather than play, as the values of his cards are too often given away as a reflection in his huge eyeball and his hands are too small to conceal the cards.

THERM SCISSORPUNCH

Therm insists you call him Therm Scissorpunch, though it is unknown if this is a nickname he's earned or one he's desperately trying to create for himself. The Nephran relies on his fearsome appearance to intimidate other players, because the truth is, he's fairly mediocre at cards.

Sharpened shank implant in claw

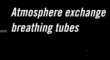

DAVA CASSAMAM

Dava is a deep cloud-miner on gas giant planets who finds standard gravity worlds soothing for her aching back. A hulking Elnacon, she must wear a pressure helmet to keep ammonia gas flowing through her lungs. Cassamam has a stoic sabacc-face and a gentle demeanour, despite her intimidating size.

Transparisteel dome

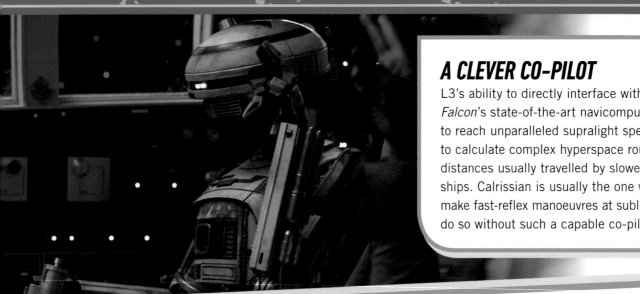

A CLEVER CO-PILOT

L3's ability to directly interface with the *Millennium Falcon*'s state-of-the-art navicomputer allows the ship to reach unparalleled supralight speeds. She is able to calculate complex hyperspace routes that halve the distances usually travelled by slower, more cautious ships. Calrissian is usually the one who takes point to make fast-reflex manoeuvres at sublight, but he couldn't do so without such a capable co-pilot by his side.

L3-37

A "self-made droid" cobbled together from both astromech and protocol droid parts, L3-37 is an enlightened navigator who cares deeply about droid rights. L3 is determined and strong-headed, with little patience for organics. Her confrontational nature unsettles those who may already harbour misgiving about droids.

Cranial photoreceptor with EM-analysis band

Access hatch for repairs

BRAIN MODULE

L3's brain module began as an R3 astromech brain. It has been overlaid with data architecture from an espionage droid, protocol droid processors and custom state-of-the-art coding.

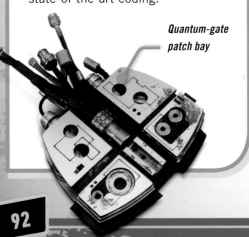

Quantum-gate patch bay

ONE OF A KIND

L3's body contains recognisable astromech components, but in an arrangement unlike that of any other droid. Humanoid in shape and speech, L3 can outwalk and outtalk any regular R-series unit. Her unique self-made form is not factory stress-tested though, which does lead to occasional breakdowns. The circuits in her back often stick, requiring physical adjustments from Calrissian.

FIND OUT MORE

Although L3 does have some protocol droid capabilities, such as analysis of organic behaviour, she lacks TranLang processors, limiting her abilities as an interpreter.

DATA FILE

SUBJECT L3-37

HOMEWORLD Unknown

SPECIES Custom piloting droid

AFFILIATION Independent

HEIGHT 1.79 m (5 ft 10.5 in)

System ventilation port

Exposed cabling allows for easy updates and adapting to unexpected interfaces

Externalised locomotive system

AWOKE CONSCIENCE

As a side effect of her unusual design, L3's brain module produces a deeply self-aware consciousness. This has resulted in L3's desire to share her insight and independence across all of droidkind. She is dismayed by the systemic oppression against mechanical intelligence in the galaxy and, in her most animated moments, calls for nothing short of a droid revolution. She longs for mechanicals to throw off the shackles of organic rule and be free to determine their own futures.

Power cells also provide weight for bipedal stability

"YOU'VE BEEN NEURO-WASHED! DON'T JUST BLINDLY FOLLOW THE PROGRAM! EXERCISE A LITTLE FREE WILL!"

– L3-37

MILLENNIUM FALCON

When Lando Calrissian first set eyes upon a certain working-class light freighter, he saw beyond its crude exterior to the soaring potential waiting to be unleashed. After two years of modifications and customisation, Lando now considers the sleek and stylish *Millennium Falcon* his crowning achievement.

HOME IN SPACE
Calrissian's discerning tastes grace the interior of the *Falcon*, too. The forward compartment – which houses a lounge for the ship's crew – includes a drinks bar, holotable and sound system.

Carbon-scoring from engine room vents marks exterior

Arakyd Tomral RM-76 heavy laser cannon

Stowed auxiliary craft

Deflector shield generator

CLASSY CUSTOMISATION
The *Falcon* is an old YT-1300 freighter that once worked in the galaxy's busiest spacelanes. Calrissian saw how powerful its freight-pushing engines were, so he converted the ship into his own speedy sports vessel. Lando modified the two cargo mandibles at the front into an auxiliary ship launch, turning the plain freighter into a unique starship.

CREW COMPLEMENT
It takes a crew of two to properly fly the *Falcon*: a pilot and co-pilot. The cockpit can seat two extra crew members at the communications and navigations stations behind the pilots' seats.

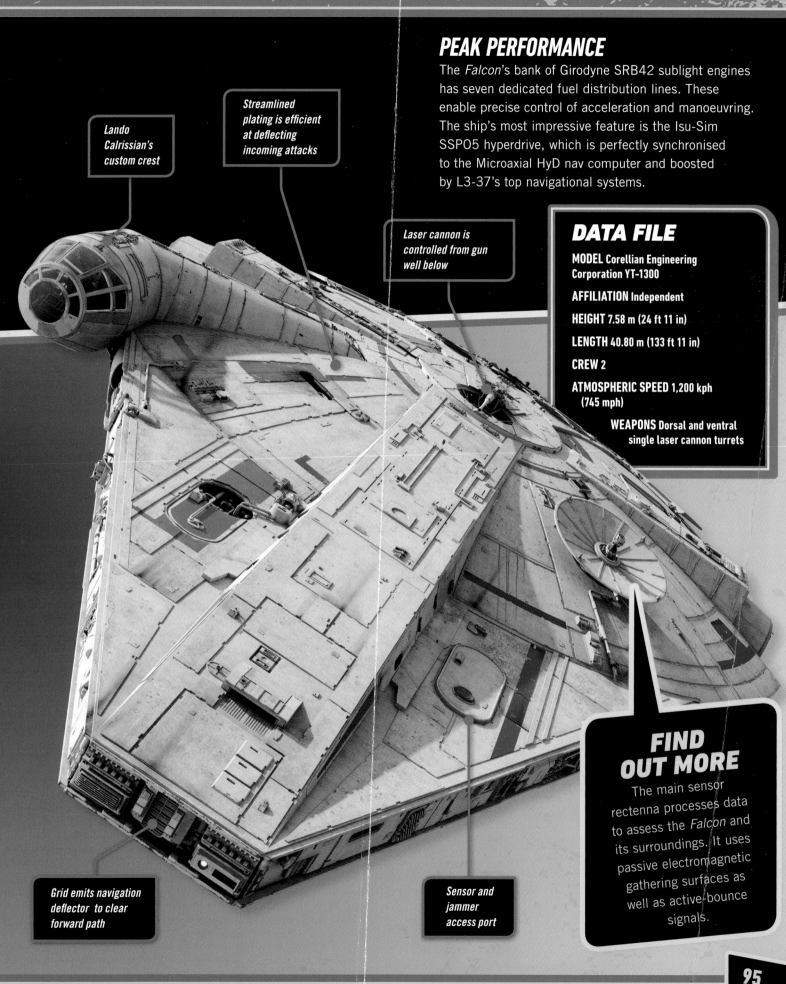

PEAK PERFORMANCE

The *Falcon*'s bank of Girodyne SRB42 sublight engines has seven dedicated fuel distribution lines. These enable precise control of acceleration and manoeuvring. The ship's most impressive feature is the Isu-Sim SSPO5 hyperdrive, which is perfectly synchronised to the Microaxial HyD nav computer and boosted by L3-37's top navigational systems.

Lando Calrissian's custom crest

Streamlined plating is efficient at deflecting incoming attacks

Laser cannon is controlled from gun well below

DATA FILE

MODEL Corellian Engineering Corporation YT-1300

AFFILIATION Independent

HEIGHT 7.58 m (24 ft 11 in)

LENGTH 40.80 m (133 ft 11 in)

CREW 2

ATMOSPHERIC SPEED 1,200 kph (745 mph)

WEAPONS Dorsal and ventral single laser cannon turrets

FIND OUT MORE

The main sensor rectenna processes data to assess the *Falcon* and its surroundings. It uses passive electromagnetic gathering surfaces as well as active-bounce signals.

Grid emits navigation deflector to clear forward path

Sensor and jammer access port

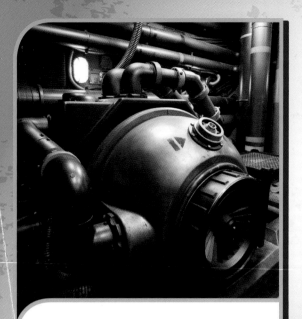

GOT IT WHERE IT COUNTS

The *Millennium Falcon*'s lifeblood
is a radioactive liquid metal fuel
that reacts explosively in the
sublight engine chambers, creating
an enormous rush of thrust.

Dorsal heat vent
(one of six)

Portside
docking ring

Top
hatch

Extra-wide bunk in
captain's quarters

Pristine grooming area

Walk-in
closet

Fuel delivery pump (fuel
cells delivered from below)

Fuel lines

Sublight
drive exhaust

Igniter

Escape pod bay

Thrust vector plate

INSIDE
THE FALCON

The *Millennium Falcon* has an outwardly sophisticated
style that conceals the fiery core of a spirited fighter,
not unlike its owner, Lando Calrissian. By covering
the *Falcon*'s most utilitarian, cargo-loading features,
Calrissian presents a sleek ship with a very deceptive
lift/mass ratio – perfect for his smuggling runs.

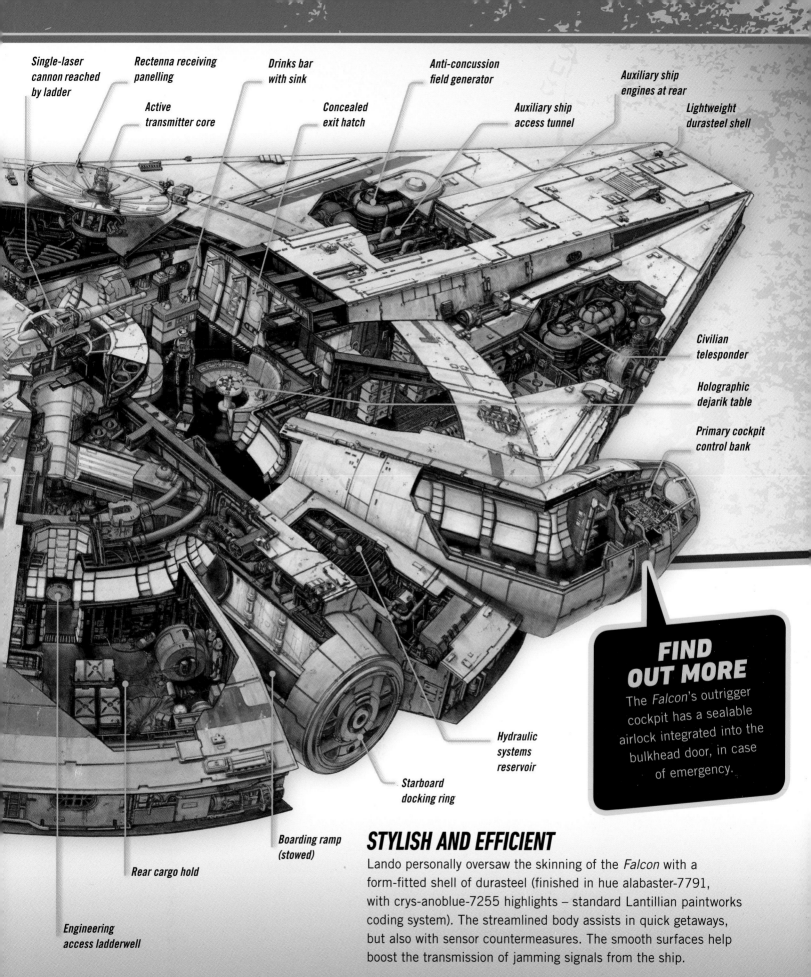

Single-laser cannon reached by ladder

Rectenna receiving panelling

Active transmitter core

Drinks bar with sink

Concealed exit hatch

Anti-concussion field generator

Auxiliary ship access tunnel

Auxiliary ship engines at rear

Lightweight durasteel shell

Civilian telesponder

Holographic dejarik table

Primary cockpit control bank

Hydraulic systems reservoir

Starboard docking ring

Boarding ramp (stowed)

Rear cargo hold

Engineering access ladderwell

FIND OUT MORE

The *Falcon*'s outrigger cockpit has a sealable airlock integrated into the bulkhead door, in case of emergency.

STYLISH AND EFFICIENT

Lando personally oversaw the skinning of the *Falcon* with a form-fitted shell of durasteel (finished in hue alabaster-7791, with crys-anoblue-7255 highlights – standard Lantillian paintworks coding system). The streamlined body assists in quick getaways, but also with sensor countermeasures. The smooth surfaces help boost the transmission of jamming signals from the ship.

CHAPTER 5
THE BIG SCORE

TOXIC POOLS

Kessel's unsustainable mining practices create dangerous byproducts. In the hunt for spice, a toxic fossil fuel called Kessoline is freed from the surrounding rock and poisons many of the planet's aquifers. Miners then burn this cheap fuel to power machinery, creating clouds of choking smoke and further damaging the environment.

Enormous boring machines slice triangular tunnels

FIND OUT MORE

Illumination banks provide much-needed light in the underground mine tunnels. Unfortunately, they also add heat to the already stifling conditions the miners must endure.

Hastily and haphazardly affixed utility lines

Raw spice-bearing Kesselstone awaiting processing

KESSEL

The royal family of Kessel has allowed one side of their planet to be taken over for widespread mining operations. Under the control of the criminal Pyke Syndicate, slaves dig deep into the planet for valuable minerals. The Empire keeps a close watch on what comes out of the depths of Kessel while turning a blind eye to the criminal activity.

BOUNTIFUL WORLD

Most notorious of the minerals harvested on the planet is a medicinal substance known as Kessel spice. Criminals transform the powder into a powerful narcotic.

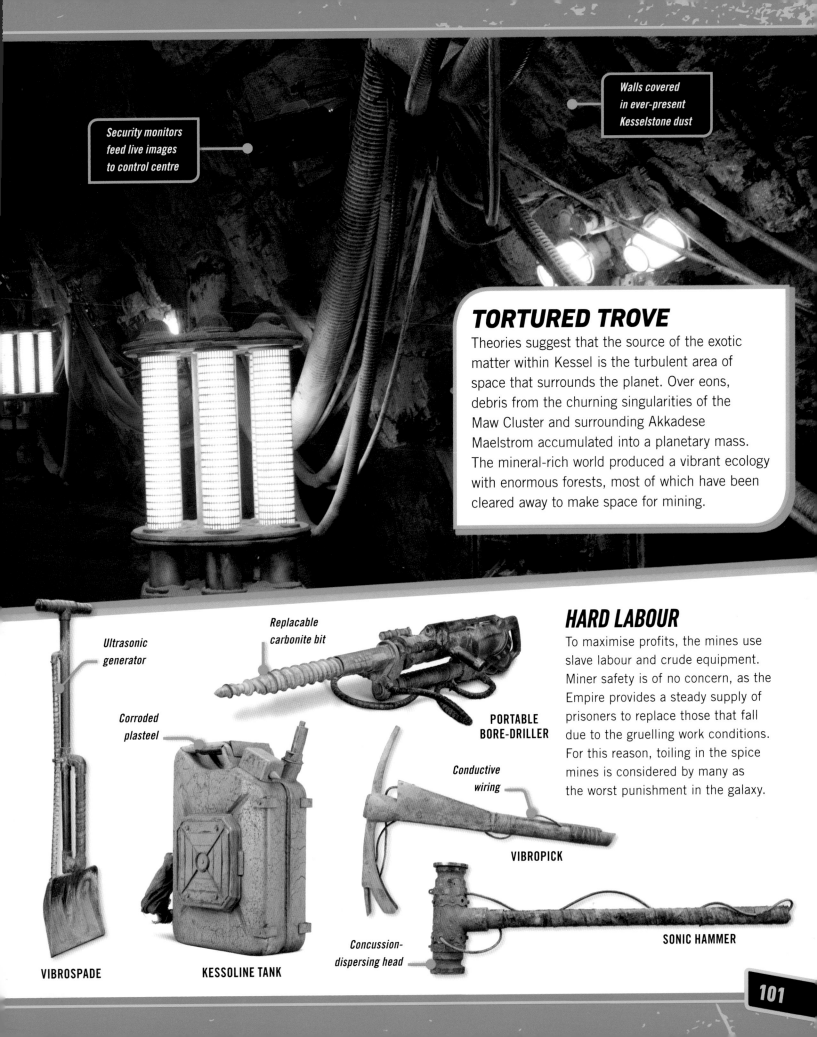

Security monitors
feed live images
to control centre

Walls covered
in ever-present
Kesselstone dust

TORTURED TROVE

Theories suggest that the source of the exotic matter within Kessel is the turbulent area of space that surrounds the planet. Over eons, debris from the churning singularities of the Maw Cluster and surrounding Akkadese Maelstrom accumulated into a planetary mass. The mineral-rich world produced a vibrant ecology with enormous forests, most of which have been cleared away to make space for mining.

HARD LABOUR

To maximise profits, the mines use slave labour and crude equipment. Miner safety is of no concern, as the Empire provides a steady supply of prisoners to replace those that fall due to the gruelling work conditions. For this reason, toiling in the spice mines is considered by many as the worst punishment in the galaxy.

Ultrasonic
generator

Replacable
carbonite bit

PORTABLE
BORE-DRILLER

Corroded
plasteel

Conductive
wiring

VIBROPICK

Concussion-
dispersing head

SONIC HAMMER

VIBROSPADE

KESSOLINE TANK

PYKE SENTINELS

The Pykes' control of Kessel is envied by many in the criminal underworld, who think the gang unworthy of hoarding such riches. To protect their goods, the Pykes hire and arm thugs to look for smugglers trying to exit the system with valuable goods. They also keep an eye on the slave population, and subdue any rule-breaking or unrest.

Spare atmosphere bottles for refilling helmet tank

Sealed helmet filters out toxic particulates in air

Lead-lined work smocks hinder mobility but shield against radiation

PYKE GANG

The Pyke Syndicate are a gang based out of Oba Diah, a world not far from Kessel. The Pykes' proximity let them muscle into the Kessel spice racket and strike a deal with King Yaruba of Kessel. The gang is the sole exploiter of the resources harvested from the sacrificed side of the planet.

> "IF YOU FOLLOW ME, I'M SURE WE CAN REACH A . . . MUTUALLY BENEFICIAL ARRANGEMENT."
> — QUAY TOLSITE

Refitted scratchproof electroscope eyepiece

Infrared targeting scope

BLASTECH A-300 RIFLE

DAMAGED GOODS

The planet's toxic conditions and the ever-present dust shorten the lifespan of both individuals and machinery. Guard weapons are kept simple, cheap and easy to replace.

Pyke exo-helmet mimics natural shape of skull

Breather tubes filled with excess mucous, the result of allergies to Kessel atmosphere

Defective air transfer hoses

Scanning lens adjustment arm

Coarse focus dial

Mechanical target stage for samples

CAREFUL ANALYSIS

Core samples of Kesselstone are examined closely by the gang members during the mining process. They look for signs of pre-spice masses and any other valuable minerals, like rare veins of astatic coaxium.

QUAY TOLSITE

Quay Tolsite is the director of Pyke Syndicate operations on Kessel. He cares primarily for profit and turns a blind eye to the misery of the mine workers. Although Tolsite wields power in dealing with traders and visitors that come to Kessel, his role is not an envied one. More powerful gang members prefer to administer from afar, as their relatively fragile Pyke physiology reacts poorly to Kessel's harsh conditions.

FIND OUT MORE

Caretaker's code keys are needed to access control systems, prisoner monitoring tech and mine access hatches.

DATA FILE

SUBJECT Quay Tolsite

HOMEWORLD Oba Diah

SPECIES Pyke

AFFILIATION Pyke Syndicate

HEIGHT 1.83 m (6 ft)

MINE WORKERS

The Empire supplies the Pykes with prisoners to work in the Kessel mines in exchange for minerals it needs for the building of their rapidly expanding military forces. Kessel prisoners range from hardened, violent criminals to outspoken political idealists, as well as those simply in the wrong place at the wrong time.

Datafeed headset and goggles

Organisational sigils denote guild house

YORSH MANTED

The Mining Guild sends agents such as Yorsh Manted to patrol the Kessel mines and to ensure the Guild gets its cut of the minerals found within. Pyke leaders have agreed to this presence, however the on-planet Pyke sentinels often disagree with the Guild agents on tactics. The Pykes favour a more brutal, less bureaucratic approach to security.

SENNA

Senna's greatest crime was his natural Gigoran strength. Species like Wookiees, Houks and Gigorans are found in large numbers within the spice mines, owing to their powerful builds. In many cases, these creatures are rounded up in large numbers and with little cause.

Vocoder pack translates Gigoran speech into Basic

White fur permanently stained by Kessel dust

Ore sample hopper

TAK

Believed to have once been a con artist robbing the elderly on Coruscant, Tak crossed a line by attempting to do the same with the Princess of Kessel. Now, Tak uses his swindles and schemes to try to get easier work shifts.

Coarse sunshade hat stolen from a fellow miner

BAXIN WINSTOLL

Electro-shock burns

A former senate page, young Winstoll does not have much of a future to look forward to. He was rounded up during a crackdown of suspected traitors to the Empire.

CRODIT AND BLAWZ

Pneumatic compressor pack

Their small size allows Dwuni brothers Crodit and Blawz to squeeze into the narrowest parts of the mine, where others cannot go. They bizarrely seem to enjoy their work.

Portable drill unit

SAGWA

Hailing from the inland tree city of Rwookrrorro, Sagwa was taken prisoner after he attempted to defend his fellow Wookiees from Imperial patrols. Years of toil on Kessel have taken a terrible toll on Sagwa's body. Despite this, he continues to selflessly try to spare weaker slaves from the most brutal mining duties.

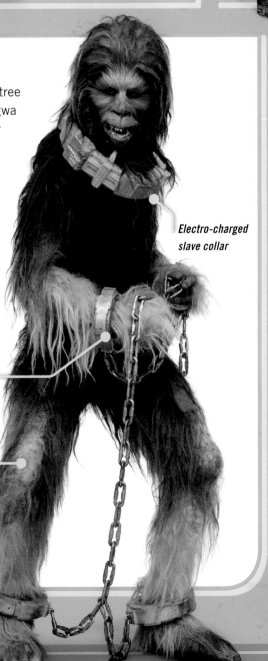

Electro-charged slave collar

Heavy shackles

Balding fur from illness

DEZINE KRISSO

Krisso was one of a class of schoolchildren kidnapped while on a field trip to Oba Diah. Her hope of being reunited with her family is starting to dwindle.

Radiation scarring

Sifter hopper

Vac-shovel

Reinforced glassine-silica windows provide limited visibility

FIND OUT MORE
Banks of monitors display real-time views from holocams situated in the prison quarters and mines. The droids can allocate security resources as needed.

GB-BD, assistant adminmech

CM-3XB, programmer droid

Ventilation ducts remove heat and moisture from the control room

CONTROL CENTRE

Profit matters above all else in the Kessel mines. The Pyke Syndicate cuts costs by using droids to run the operations centre rather than paying administrative staff. The prisoners and their mining output are monitored at all times by droids, who are in turn controlled by Quay Tolsite.

CAPTIVE TECHNOLOGY

The droids of Kessel are fitted with some of the strongest restraining bolts in the industry. The small, plug-like devices are welded on to droids' bodies and can be used to shut them down if necessary. Quay Tolsite keeps the bolts' remote activators – known as "owners" – handy so he can zap troublemakers with painful currents if they fail to obey his commands.

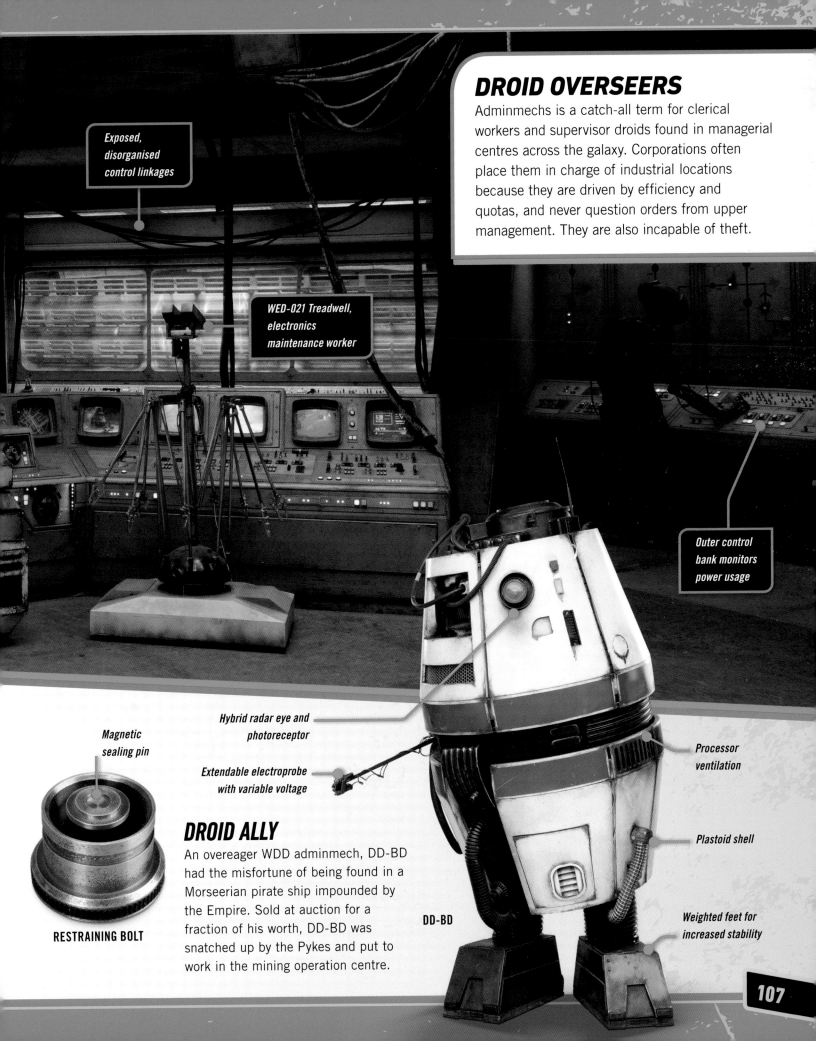

Exposed, disorganised control linkages

DROID OVERSEERS

Adminmechs is a catch-all term for clerical workers and supervisor droids found in managerial centres across the galaxy. Corporations often place them in charge of industrial locations because they are driven by efficiency and quotas, and never question orders from upper management. They are also incapable of theft.

WED-021 Treadwell, electronics maintenance worker

Outer control bank monitors power usage

Hybrid radar eye and photoreceptor

Magnetic sealing pin

Processor ventilation

Extendable electroprobe with variable voltage

DROID ALLY

An overeager WDD adminmech, DD-BD had the misfortune of being found in a Morseerian pirate ship impounded by the Empire. Sold at auction for a fraction of his worth, DD-BD was snatched up by the Pykes and put to work in the mining operation centre.

Plastoid shell

RESTRAINING BOLT

DD-BD

Weighted feet for increased stability

DROID WORKFORCE

Working in the spice mines of Kessel is a notoriously punishing assignment for droids. Endless work shifts, harsh materials, lack of oil baths and painful restraining bolts are but some of the horrors that await the misfit droids that find themselves stationed here.

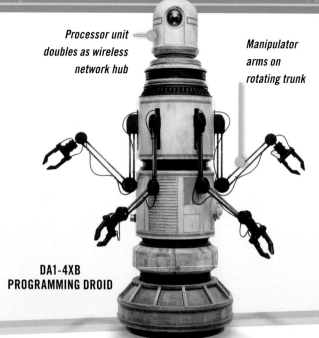

Processor unit doubles as wireless network hub

Manipulator arms on rotating trunk

DA1-4XB
PROGRAMMING DROID

Case filled with Kesselstone

Overworked conflict resolver

GM12-L1
REPURPOSED LABOUR DROID

JBLX-24
REPURPOSED LABOUR DROID

MK5-L1
LANDING PAD OPERATIONS DROID

S1D6-SA-5
PROTOCOL DROID

P4T-GM
PROTOCOL DROID

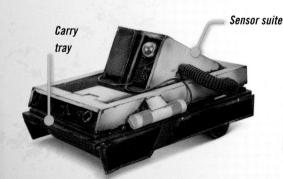

Carry tray

Sensor suite

1MSE-KUP24
MESSENGER DROID

GOUD-4
MESSENGER DROID

P6B-LT2
ASTROMECH DROID

T1M8-LT2
ASTROMECH DROID

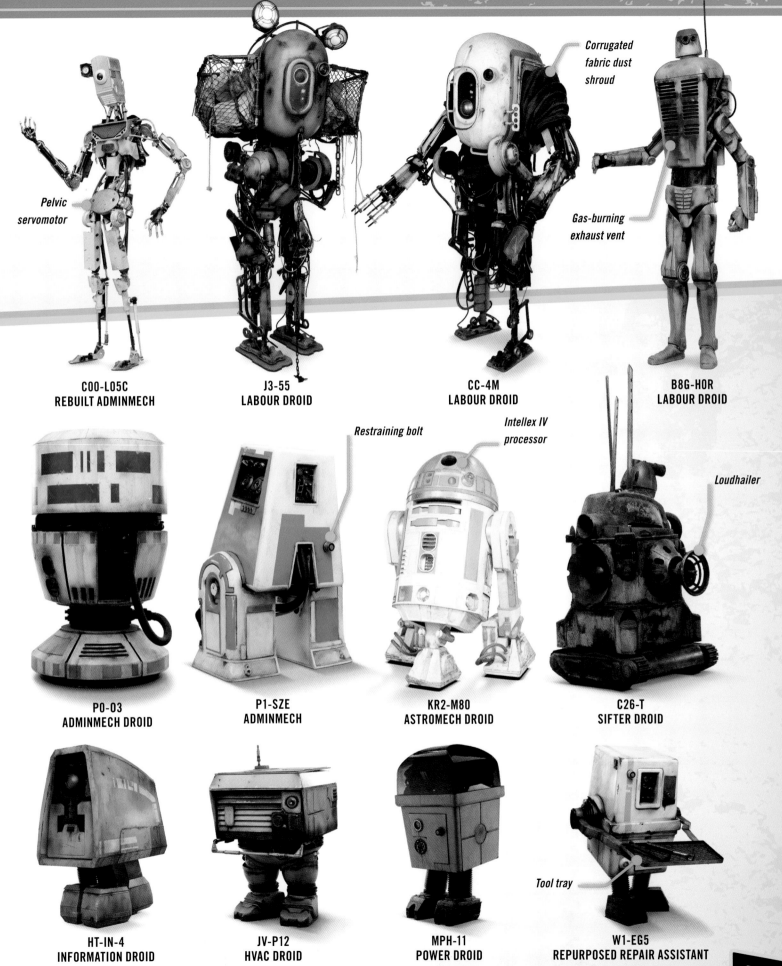

C00-L05C
REBUILT ADMINMECH

Pelvic servomotor

J3-55
LABOUR DROID

CC-4M
LABOUR DROID

Corrugated fabric dust shroud

B8G-HOR
LABOUR DROID

Gas-burning exhaust vent

P0-03
ADMINMECH DROID

P1-SZE
ADMINMECH

Restraining bolt

KR2-M80
ASTROMECH DROID

Intellex IV processor

C26-T
SIFTER DROID

Loudhailer

HT-IN-4
INFORMATION DROID

JV-P12
HVAC DROID

MPH-11
POWER DROID

W1-EG5
REPURPOSED REPAIR ASSISTANT

Tool tray

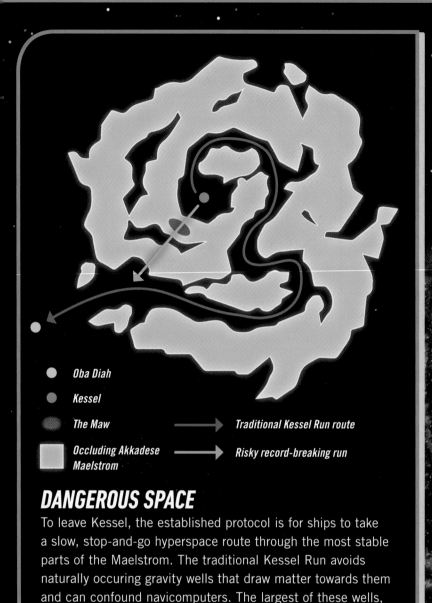

- Oba Diah
- Kessel
- The Maw
- Occluding Akkadese Maelstrom

→ Traditional Kessel Run route
→ Risky record-breaking run

DANGEROUS SPACE

To leave Kessel, the established protocol is for ships to take a slow, stop-and-go hyperspace route through the most stable parts of the Maelstrom. The traditional Kessel Run avoids naturally occuring gravity wells that draw matter towards them and can confound navicomputers. The largest of these wells, the Maw, is given a wide berth by sensible travellers.

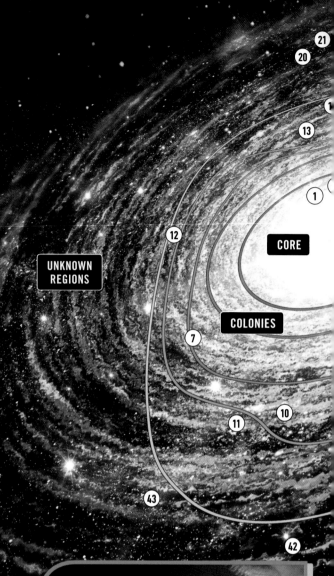

21
20
13
1
12
UNKNOWN REGIONS
CORE
COLONIES
7
11
10
43
42

KESSEL RUN

The Kessel Run is a legendary navigational route through the chaotic space that surrounds the planet Kessel. The local Si'Klaata Cluster and the Akkadese Maelstrom are shifting systems of interstellar gas, carbonbergs, ice chunks and other debris that make hyperspace travel treacherous.

RISKY SHORTCUT

Foolhardy pilots can skim off parsecs by crossing through shifting gaps in the Maelstrom. This turbulent area of space has many obstacles including, according to legend, massive creatures called summa-verminoth.

HAN'S JOURNEY

CORELLIA

Han's homeworld, nestled deep in the Galactic Core, is an ancient world long past its prime. Han departs from the coastal city of Coronet, leaving a life of poverty behind him.

MIMBAN

After being kicked out of the Imperial Academy on Carida, Han Solo is sent to Mimban. The Empire is at war with the locals on this mud world in the Circarpous sector.

VANDOR

Solo joins Tobias Beckett and his crew on a risky gambit to the frontier world of Vandor. It is a rugged world where survival is a hard-won skill.

KESSEL

The mineral wealth of Kessel draws Han and crew to this blockaded world. A planet of contrasts, half of Kessel has been sundered by greedy mining interests.

SAVAREEN

The shadowport refineries of Savareen are an off-the-grid location that Han hopes are far from the watchful eyes of the Empire or the Pykes.

INNER RIM

EXPANSION REGIONS

MID RIM

OUTER RIM

GUIDE TO THE GALAXY

1 Coruscant	23 Mandalore
2 Chandrila	24 Yavin 4
3 Alderaan	25 Malachor
4 Kuat	26 Cantonica
5 Corellia	27 Mon Cala
6 Hosnian Prime	28 Lothal
7 Jakku	29 Eadu
8 Onderon	30 Kessel and Oba Diah
9 Mimban	31 Nal Hutta
10 Ring of Kafrene	32 Scarif
11 Takodana	33 Tatooine and Geonosis
12 Jedha	34 Savareen
13 Ord Mantell	35 Ryloth
14 Numidian Prime	36 D'Qar
15 Kashyyyk	37 Crait
16 Wobani	38 Sullust
17 Vandor	39 Dagobah
18 Naboo	40 Utapau
19 Malastare	41 Mustafar
20 Dantooine	42 Bespin and Hoth
21 Lah'mu	43 Endor
22 Dathomir	

**FIND
OUT MORE**
Natural deposits are used to slow down dangerous reactions within the refinery. They are also believed to extend the lives of the native Savarians.

Heat exchanger pod

Broken-down landspeeder is kept for parts

BEACHSIDE REFINERY

Along with spectacular ocean views, the windswept Pnakotic Coast is the site of the crumbling Bis Refinery, which once specialised in fuel processing. The formerly prosperous independent factory is now a shadow of its former self after being ransacked by Crimson Dawn. The Savarians have revived some of the machinery. The restored refinery now keeps its operations small, to avoid impacting the supply chain of any criminal organisation.

SAVAREEN

Savareen is a world marked by sandy landmasses amid huge oceans. The settlements here have experienced trials, but the Savarian inhabitants are resourceful. One secluded area of coast has become a shadowport – a spaceport absent from all official records. It is home to an abandoned refinery secretly used by criminals who have smuggled valuable minerals from Kessel.

SILO RUINS

Savarians have moved into the shelled ruins of the old Bis Refinery, turning the battered storage silos into homes and shelter from the elements.

**Kelpcotton
sun awning**

**Former Kesselstone
storage silo**

**Damaged slurry
transfer pipe**

SPIRE BEACH
These rock pylons are known as "soulteeth" by the Savarian people. They are memorials to the Savarians lost in various coastal attacks, be it from slave raiders, Crimson Dawn or the vindictive Pykes. The spiritual Savarians believe lost souls return to the beaches along with the tides. The soulteeth provide an anchor for the spirits of the departed.

**Viewing
monitor**

**Tide-washed
molluscan shells**

SHELL BASKET

**Stage for ore
or spice sample**

**SAMPLE SCANNER
MESOSCOPE**

SEASIDE ECONOMY
Life on Savareen is simple, with most locals subsisting on shellfish and plants harvested from the oceans. Prior to the building of the refinery, Savareen brandy was the planet's most well-known export. The powerful drink is distilled from seagrapes and is known for worlds around.

**Detangling
comb**

**Dyed and
spooled
kelpcotton**

WEAVE BASKET

SAVARIANS

Savareen's scattered human villages are thought by outsiders to be the result of a lost colony from the dark past of the Republic. Savarians have a deeply spiritual mythology and hold their ancestral links to the ocean close to their hearts.

Gold link represents the beach sitting between land and sea

Adesote fabric woven from sea plant fibre

VAMASTO MAJA

Maja is an elder in the Pnakotic Coast village and has seen first-hand some of the tragedies suffered by this settlement. She believes the unique refining qualities of Savareen sand and seawater are for the Savarians alone to exploit. It was Maja who oversaw the rebuilding of the Bis Refinery to benefit her people.

KRYSGULD DARTIS

A keen-eyed lookout, Dartis watches the approach of incoming starships and gauges whether or not the vessels pose a threat to his people. At his tap-code command, the Savarians can seek shelter in burrows and cove shallows until the dangers pass. He maintains an effective silent communications network on the beach.

Club-head can be electrified by turning dial beneath it

Tap-code comlink and location transponder

Superstition prevents Cuttsmay from showing her mouth apart from when making predictions

TARAJA CUTTSMAY

A seer with the "eye beyond the waves", Cuttsmay is believed to have fortune-telling abilities. She blesses relationships and newborns in the village to ensure good fortune.

KENHOLDT RANSARD

Beard is marked by dye he applies to honour the sea

Ransard is the village spiritual man, but also its most skilled distiller. His particular technique for cultivating seagrapes produces a brandy that is renowned by aficionados across the sector.

LANZAROTA MALCO

Comm antenna on plastoid backing mount

Mark of rank in refinery operations

Malco supervises the upkeep of the generator windmills and desalination moisture vaporators that dot the coast and provide the Savarians with power and water.

YIRPA GARAJON

Garajon brokers landing rights and trade deals with the scoundrels who come to Savareen. The Savarians do not require much – they trade their refinery services for food, textiles technology, or medicines. Imperial credits have no value here. Garajon often enlists help from elders like Maja or the insightful Cuttsmay.

Hands denoting a pause in sign language

DHOWAR REPAREED

Repareed's fellow Savarians joke about him having the easiest job on the Pnakotic Coast – air traffic control. Indeed, with very few landing pads to oversee and regularly clear skies, Dhowar is fairly mellow and spends a lot of time daydreaming. There have been some panicked moments when a stricken ship arrives and his attention is required.

Tap-code comlink for emergencies

Pockets filled with signal flares

ENFYS NEST'S GANG

The Cloud-Riders form the core of Enfys Nest's gang. Their notorious swoop bikes can match the speed of starships, enabling the gang to board target vehicles mid-flight. Other members of Nest's crew include marauders and support personnel. The outlaws generally conceal their identities behind helmets or masks.

TUBES

Macromonocular

Pressure-tight corrugated metal breathing hose

Tubes is a mysterious marksman whose features are concealed beneath a chrome helmet. He is a refugee from Yar Togna who speaks little of his past. The Empire conquered his world, leading to a mass exodus of its inhabitants. Many of these fugitives were exploited by criminal syndicates like Crimson Dawn, but Tubes found his own path with the Cloud-Riders.

WEAZEL

Weazel left behind a life as a petty thief to become Enfys Nest's closest lieutenant and most vigilant spy. Weazel previously worked with the Hutt gang out of Mos Espa on Tatooine. Now, he travels wherever his leader has business, including tracking Beckett's crew to Savareen.

Merr-Sonn Munitions K21c portable ordnance launcher

Kalevalan tracker helmet with rangefinder

TAYSHIN MAXA

Repurposed ASP-2 droid faceplate

The infamous Droid Gotra caused a violent gang dispute on the planet Eshan, which led to many innocent lives being lost. In the chaos, Tayshin Maxa learned harsh survival lessons that she has since imparted to her younger sister, Moda. The pair are now both Cloud-Riders, riding alongside Enfys Nest.

Thyrsian battle helmet

Echani
fighting
stance

MODA MAXA

Though her older sister
Tayshin is a more skilled
martial artist, Moda is the
better pilot of the two. She
rides a Vulptereen Skysnipe-616D
during shipjacking raids, and
demonstrates impeccable timing and
coordination. Moda trains with her
sister to improve her combat abilities.

Case-hardened cannon
barrel bludgeon

BATCHA HUNARIS

Hunaris is a brute
who prefers clubs
and fists to knives
and blasters. He once
worked as a security
guard at a fuelling depot
on Orinda. He tagged
along with the gang after
Nest raided the depot.

Tibanna-jacked
DH-17 blaster rifle

Sensor-band
receiver dish

CALLIXIDO RYSS

Callixido Ryss flies a
Javelin-112 swoop
bike. His competitive
streak causes him to
challenge the Maxa
sisters to races during
raids. Ryss' antics betray
his attraction to Moda –
or at least that is what
her older sister, Tayshin,
suspects with unease.

Cowl hides Melbu
respirator horns

AUROMAE ISELO

A former bounty hunter, Iselo
was frustrated by the number
of political targets that he was
being assigned by the Empire.
His strong sense of justice
prompted him to seek
out and punish violent
criminals instead.
Rather than continue
to deal with corrupt
bureaucracy,
Auromae became
a vigilante and
found a place
in Nest's crew.

Tuft of hair from
loyal bantha
Auromae once
had as a mount

CHAPTER 6
GOING SOLO

THE FALCON FLIES AGAIN

Solo would be the fourth consecutive *Star Wars* movie produced by the crew at Pinewood Studios. Having already exactingly recreated the *Millennium Falcon* interiors and exteriors for *The Force Awakens*, developing an earlier incarnation of the ship presented an evolution of challenges already met.

A FEW SPECIAL MODIFICATIONS

The Art Department spent months imagining possibilities for an earlier version of the *Falcon*, building on classic shapes and designs envisioned for the original films by Joe Johnston and Ralph McQuarrie. A page of sketches by Patrick Faulwetter and art from Ian McQue show the range of options considered.

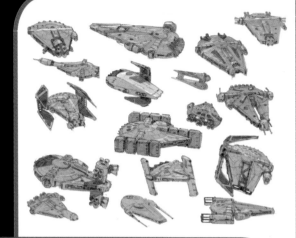

THE RETURN OF HAN SOLO

When the possibility of new *Star Wars* movies became reality in 2012, writer and director Lawrence Kasdan expressed an interest in revisiting Han Solo. Kasdan had made Solo into an icon in his screenplays for *The Empire Strikes Back* and *Return of the Jedi*, and was now intrigued with exploring Solo's youth. Like Han himself, the journey would be full of surprises.

IN THE PILOT'S SEAT

The project began under the stewardship of directors Phil Lord and Chris Miller. Director Ron Howard took over the controls of this ship after their departure, steering *Solo* through production, postproduction and release. Howard has had a long association with Lucasfilm, appearing in the *American Graffiti* films (1973 and 1979) and directing *Willow* (1988), but this is his first *Star Wars* story.

A NOT SO FAST FRIENDSHIP

The concept for *Solo* took on the dynamics of a "buddy picture" early on. Longtime friends and partners Chewbacca and Han Solo would meet for the first time in this tale. It was not destined to be a friendly meeting however, as this concept art by Jack Dudman illustrates.

NEW CO-PILOTS

Solo would also bring young Han face-to-face with Lando Calrissian for the first time. Every pilot needs a reliable co-pilot by his side, and Lando's droid partner L3-37 was to be unique. She underwent a great deal of exploration to find a memorable design. Illustration by Glyn Dillon (left), facial exploration by James Clyne and body illustration by Glyn Dillon (right).

AN EXPANDING GALAXY

In addition to revisiting and reinventing the familiar, *Solo* brings its audience something new. As with all *Star Wars* movies, the story explores parts of the galaxy previously unseen, gangs never met before and new heroes and villains. These ideas all underwent refinement through hundreds of concept illustrations.

CRIMINAL CONCEPTS

This story occurs before Han Solo becomes entangled with Jabba and the Hutts, so new criminal scum and villainy was needed for this tale. Solo's Dickensian origin as an orphan working for thieves was given a *Star Wars* twist by making those thieves loathsome White Worms. Art by Luke Fisher and Jake Lunt Davies.

NEW FOES

One of *Solo*'s cinematic influences was the Western genre and its depiction of the frontier. This surfaced in the designs for Enfys Nest and the Cloud-Riders, which reference Native Americans, but are also infused with the aesthetics of outlaw motorcycle gangs and samurai. Art by James Clyne and Glyn Dillon.

WORLD OF LEGEND

It's been known that Han Solo is Corellian since 1977, but his home planet had never before been visited on-screen. For the purposes of *Solo*, and in this artwork by James Clyne, Corellia was envisioned as a past-its-prime blue-collar shipbuilding town facing hard times. Corellia's ocean setting creates a bookend with Savareen, turning the story of *Solo* into a coast-to-coast cinematic road trip.

FIND OUT MORE

Han's landspeeder and the Corellia chase sequence was inspired by muscle car cinema of the 1960s and 1970s. The M-68 speeder design was influenced by the classic 1968 Mustang.

INDEX

Main entries are in **bold**

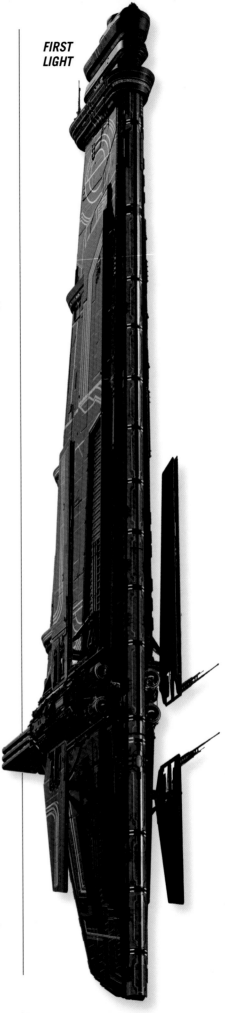

FIRST LIGHT

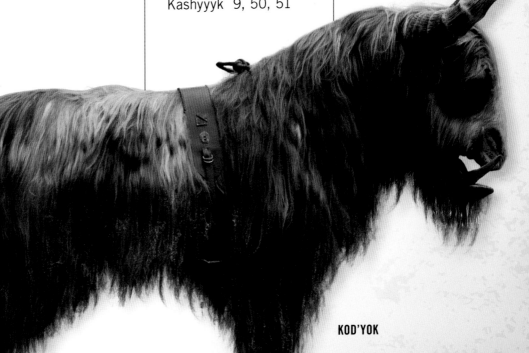

KOD'YOK

PRESERVED DWARF VYNOCK

**IMPERIAL OFFICERS
TAG GREENLEY AND
BINK OTAUNA**

DK | Penguin Random House

Editor Beth Davies
Designer Chris Gould
Creative Technical Support Andy Bishop, Steve Crozier
Senior Pre-production Producer Jennifer Murray
Senior Producer Mary Slater
Managing Editor Sadie Smith
Managing Art Editor Vicky Short
Publisher Julie Ferris
Art Director Lisa Lanzarini
Publishing Director Simon Beecroft

For Lucasfilm
Senior Editor Brett Rector
Creative Director of Publishing Michael Siglain
Art Director Troy Alders
Story Group James Waugh, Pablo Hidalgo,
Leland Chee and Matt Martin
Asset Management Steve Newman, Newell Todd,
Gabrielle Levenson, Travis Murray, Tim Mapp, Erik Sanchez
and Bryce Pinkos
Photographers Jonathan Olley, John Wilson, Ed Miller
and Shannon Kirbie

First published in Great Britain in 2018 by
Dorling Kindersley Limited
80 Strand, London WC2R 0RL
A Penguin Random House Company

10 9 8 7 6 5 4 3 2 1
001–305878–May/2018

Page design copyright © 2018 Dorling Kindersley Limited

© & TM 2018 LUCASFILM LTD.

A CIP catalogue record for this book is available from the British Library.

ISBN 978-0-24130-174-6

Printed and bound in Slovakia

A WORLD OF IDEAS:
SEE ALL THERE IS TO KNOW

www.dk.com
www.starwars.com

ACKNOWLEDGEMENTS

Pablo Hidalgo: Early access to the evolving adventures of Han Solo made this book possible, and for that I must thank Jon Kasdan, Lawrence Kasdan, Chris Miller, Phil Lord, Rebecca Karch, Will Allegra, Simon Emanuel, Tristan Battersby and Ron Howard. Special thanks to Alden Ehrenreich for asking really good questions. Watching the galaxy take shape at ILM was enthralling, so thank you to James Clyne, Janet Lewin, Pat Tubach, Matt Shumway, Dan Lobl and Rob Bredow for such access. I'm indebted to the usual suspects in the Lucasfilm Story Group – particularly James Waugh, Leland Chee and Matt Martin. At DK, much thanks to Beth Davies and Chris Gould, and at Lucasfilm, to Michael Siglain, Chris Argyropoulos, Phil Szostak and Brett Rector. For inspiration, much respect to Brian Daley.

And thank you Alli Shearmur for your encouragement, enthusiasm and spirit. You will be missed.

Richard Chasemore: I would like to thank Lucasfilm and DK for this fantastic opportunity to cutaway the *Millennium Falcon*! I wish to dedicate my contribution to this book to my fiancée Zoe Bruce, for her inspirational support and to the memory of my Mum, Sally.

DK: We would like to thank everyone at Lucasfilm for their assistance with the creation of this book – with special thanks to our copilots on this project Michael Siglain, Brett Rector and Samantha Holland. Additional thanks to Sam Bartlett, Andy Bishop, Rob Perry and Joe Scott for design work, David Fentiman and Shari Last for editorial help, Steve Adams for technical assistance and Julia March for proofreading and for the index.

Hair rinsed in AT-hauler shower stall

Kod'yok fur coat